Labour and the Benn Factor

Labour and the
Benn Factor

MICHAEL COCKS

Macdonald

A Macdonald Book

Copyright © 1989 by Michael Cocks

First published in Great Britain in 1989
by Macdonald & Co (Publishers) Ltd
London & Sydney

British Library Cataloguing in Publication Data
Cocks, Michael
Labour and the Benn factor.
I. Title
941.085'092'4

ISBN 0-356-18654-7

Typeset by Fleet Graphics, Enfield, Middlesex
Printed and bound in Great Britain by
Richard Clay Ltd, Bungay, Suffolk

Macdonald & Co (Publishers) Ltd
66-73 Shoe Lane
London EC4P 4AB

A member of Maxwell Pergamon Publishing Corporation plc

CONTENTS

	Preface	7
1.	Benn Elected to Parliament	9
2.	Credentials	20
3.	Benn as Backbencher	28
4.	Opposition Spokesman 1957-64	36
5.	House of Lords: Peerage	45
6.	Ministerial Office 1964-70	55
7.	Leadership Issue	68
8.	Industry and Energy	84
9.	Backbench Bristol South-East: 1979-83	96
10.	Mandatory Reselection	104
11.	Bristol South	120
12.	Militant	129
13.	Bristol South – Retribution	138
14.	Chesterfield	147
	Appendix I	157
	Appendix II	162
	Appendix III	167
	Index	171

This book is dedicated to the people of Bristol South, and especially to my loyal supporters who stood by me to the end.

My special thanks to Stephen Crisp, Michael Hatfield, Dr Chris Roberts and Mark Trafford for help with research; and to Mrs Andrea Hertz who prepared the index.

PREFACE

'That evil is half-cured whose cause we know'
Charles Churchill, Gotham, 1764

No-one who truly cares about the democratic process and its traditions in our country can be entirely happy with the present political climate. Regardless of one's political views, it is not healthy to have a government in office for nearly ten years and with no prospect of change until 1991-92. The existence of a viable alternative government is an essential part of the democratic process.

This book has been written in an attempt to buttress the efforts of the Labour Leader Neil Kinnock. Before and during the 1988 Labour Party conference at Blackpool, Neil Kinnock has tried to drag the Party into a sense of purpose and reality. This process will continue at the forthcoming 1989 Labour Party Conference with the new policy review, buttressed by recent successes in by-elections and the European elections. This has been necessary because, for too long, Labour's standing and support has been eroded by internal wrangling and manoeuvring. It has been a manipulation that has been conducted by a comparatively small group of people. By clever and sometimes questionable tactics, this group has wielded an influence out of all proportion to its numbers.

From April 1976 I was Chief Whip of the Labour Party for nearly ten years. During my time in office a number of my Cabinet and Shadow Cabinet colleagues and I were well aware of what was going on. We worked hard to save the Party. On 15 July 1984 *The Sunday Times* published an article entitled

7

'Anatomy of a Takeover' detailing the problems I faced in my own Bristol South constituency party which led to my deselection. Immediately after the loss of the Greenwich by-election (a Labour seat since 1945), on 26 February 1987, the same newspaper published another article in which I gave my diagnosis of Labour's problems.

I am now proud and privileged to be an active member of the House of Lords. I still care deeply for the Labour Party. With more time on my hands, I have written this book as my attempt to support Neil Kinnock in what he is trying to do, not only for the Party but also for the health of democratic politics in Britain today. I have looked in depth at the activities of one Labour Party member – Anthony Wedgwood Benn. Some would say that wittingly or unwittingly he bears much of the responsibility for the deterioration that has taken place in Labour's standing in the country. Now that he has been rejected by a margin of 9 to 1 in the last leadership contest. I hope he will regard party unity as the prime objective. I am not against change, but the repeated efforts to change the Labour Party's constitution have done nothing but harm. The Labour Party is a spectrum of views, and that has to be respected if we are all to work together. But they have to be views that are constructive, aimed at a common objective, not, as they sometimes have been, destructive, deflecting the Party from its purpose.

Hopefully, traditional Labour supporters reading this book will be encouraged to play their part in the regeneration of the Party with Neil Kinnock. If any feel I have given too much detail on the machinations that have gone on I would refer them to the opening quotation. If enough people turn on these termites who have infiltrated themselves, their activities will be eradicated and the Labour Party returned to rude health.

1

BENN ELECTED TO PARLIAMENT

Bristol was a prime target for German bombers during the war. There was, apart from a great deal of light engineering, the massive aeroplane works of the Bristol Aircraft Company at Filton, and the Bristol aero engine works at Patchway. Blenheim bombers and later Beaufighter aircraft were built there, together with thousands of engines for use in other aircraft. The docks at Avonmouth – Bristol's outport – were also a target, as was Charles Hill's dockyard which turned out a stream of small naval ships such as minesweepers and corvettes.

Bristol had a large civilian population and the bombs that rained down created heavy casualties. Throughout the city, houses and even streets were missing or blackened and jagged like rotten teeth. The great shopping centre at Wine Street and Castle Street was devastated.

Battered by bombing and suffering from wartime shortages, as well as aggravated by extensive areas of prewar deprivation, Bristol reflected the landslide to Labour in the 1945 General Election. Polling was on 5 July but the announcement of the results was delayed until 26 July to allow nearly two million Service votes cast overseas to be returned home. The results were astonishing. Clement Attlee, who had been leader of the Labour Party since 1935 and Deputy Prime Minister during the wartime coalition, became Prime Minister with an overall majority of 146.

In 1945, Bristol was divided into five constituencies. Labour gained Bristol North and Bristol Central from the Conservatives. At this time there were two national political figures elected. In Bristol East there was Sir Stafford Cripps, who was to become Chancellor of the Exchequer. Sir Stafford had been the member for the constituency since 1931. His relations with the Labour Party nationally had sometimes been stormy, especially over his advocacy of support for the Popular Front against Nazi Germany. None the less, he had many good friends and supporters locally and by 1945 he was reconciled with the national party. He had rendered sterling war service as ambassador to the Soviet Union from 1940 until 1942, when he was appointed Minister of Aircraft Production in the coalition government led by Winston Churchill.

The other national figure was Colonel Oliver Stanley, the only Conservative elected in Bristol in 1945. He had previously represented Westmorland since 1924 until the dissolution of Parliament in 1945, and had wide ministerial experience. Why he should find himself in Bristol is not without interest. His predecessor in Bristol West was C.T. Culverwell, who had earned the displeasure of Bristolians by once advocating, in effect, that Britain should be supporting Hitler against the Russians rather than fighting against him. The remarks were remembered when a badly-bombed Bristol was choosing its candidates to fight the general election. Oliver Stanley was asked to stand as a Conservative candidate in his stead.

Cripps became President of the Board of Trade in Attlee's Government. In 1947 he was briefly Minister for Economic Affairs before being pitchforked into the Chancellorship of the Exchequer following Hugh Dalton's resignation over his Budget blunder, when he carelessly revealed some of his proposals in advance. Cripps grappled manfully with the desperate economic problems that faced Britain in the postwar period.

Few people today realise just what sacrifices were made to win the war. Bristol emerged from it a different city. Dilapidation was everywhere. The roads were bad and the shops that remained had little to offer their customers. In the five years that had come and gone since the June night in 1940 when the Germans first attacked the city, there had been over 550 alerts and on 77 occasions bombs fell. Nearly 1,300 people were killed and over 3,330 were injured. Throughout Britain losses amounted to 468,000 people of whom 398,000 were combatants and 70,000 were civilians. Of the civilians, over 60,000 died under bombardment in the United Kingdom, the others in far-away countries such as Malta and Malaya, or in German and Japanese internment camps.

In the euphoria of victory in Europe few bothered to take stock of the problems facing the incoming Labour Government. Only now are the real achievements of the Attlee Administration being fully and rightly understood. During the war four and a half million houses out of the thirteen million prewar stock were damaged by enemy action. Nearly half a million of these damaged houses were beyond repair, unfit for habitation. In other words, four million houses had to be repaired. The task was enormous. Our major industries had been exhausted producing war materials. Major utilities such as gas, electricity and the railways had been run on a care and maintenance basis. There was a huge backlog of essential work to be undertaken. Millions of servicemen and women were anxious to be demobilised. It is a tribute to the Labour Government that by the end of 1947 – that is, within eighteen months of coming to power – five million service men and women had been returned to civilian life without creating the kind of massive unemployment that followed the First World War.

In addition to these physical problems, the economic position was made worse by the sale of overseas assets to pay for vital food and raw materials. It meant that net income from overseas investments was less than half the prewar figure. The abrupt termination of loans from the United States only added to the pile of economic problems facing the Chancellor of the Exchequer.

Inevitably, it can easily be said with hindsight, the enormity of the economic difficulties confronting Cripps took their toll. He had earned himself the nickname of the 'Iron Chancellor' because of the austerity programmes he introduced to meet tasks facing the country. He was an austere man himself and never really fully fit. By 1950 his health was beginning to fail, and in October of that year he announced his resignation. He had performed his duties nobly, *The New York Times* paying him the tribute: 'One might almost say he saved Britain in peace as Winston Churchill did in the war.'

His subsequent retirement from the Commons meant a by-election, only eight months after the 1950 General Election had been won by Labour with a severely reduced majority. The by-election was fought in what was a new parliamentary constituency, Bristol South-East, brought about by a redistribution, but still predominantly Labour. Preliminary discussions on the choice of a new Labour candidate had already been held. Amongst early names mentioned were: Arthur Creech Jones, a former Labour Colonial Minister, who lost his Shipley (Yorkshire) seat in the General Election, Walter Farthing, previously an MP for the old Frome division, and Ted Bishop, a local councillor.

Cripps, who was to die in 1952, had a majority of 16,803 in the 1950 General Election. The by-election was therefore fought in what was seen as a 'safe' Labour seat. It was a 'plum' constituency for a Labour candidate. In those days, however, Labour aspirants had to be very careful in pushing their wares; they had not to be seen to be over-doing things, otherwise there would be an unfavourable reaction from those who carried out the selection. Letters from people who wrote 'out of the blue' inquiring about prospects of candidatures in safe or marginal seats usually finished up in the wastepaper basket. Canvassing for support, although frowned upon, did take place. But it had to be discreet, unlike today. Now we find constituency parties inviting applications from people prepared to be considered for candidature. Moreover, since the Party adopted the reselection procedure, where every Labour MP has to submit himself for reselection during a parliamentary term (meaning that others can stand against him), the dates of reselection are advertised, and names and addresses of constituency secretaries are given together with closing dates for receipt of nominations.

I mention this relatively recent development because it is undoubtedly in the worst interests of the Labour Party. Under the previous system a recommendation from someone who knew the potential candidate was usually necessary to get a nomination. A procedure, in fact, not much different from that when applying for a job. Abilities, previous experience, loyalties, all come into play. But today a selection conference is more loaded towards somebody whose main skill is in the use of words. For proof one has only to look at the predominance of university lecturers, schoolteachers, solicitors, barristers and other professions carrying university qualifications. They all have the 'gift of the gab'. There is a further hazard for the unwary at present day reselection conferences when an MP's job is on the line. It is the checklist produced by Chris Mullin – a former editor of *Tribune*, a left-wing weekly, and now MP for Sunderland South – which is published in the document 'How to Select or Reselect Your MP'. The unrepresentative and unconventional nature of this checklist will be discussed in the appendix.

The selection conference to choose the Labour candidate to succeed Cripps was held at the Walter Baker Hall, headquarters of the Bristol South-East Labour Party, on 2 November. Ted Bishop, by this time, had stated he was not interested, having already been chosen as the Labour candidate for Exeter, while Walter Farthing was not pursued. There were three candidates' names before the meeting: Arthur Creech Jones, Mrs M.E. Nichol and Anthony Neil Wedgwood Benn.

Creech Jones had had a very distinguished career, having been National Secretary of the Transport and General Workers' Union from 1919-29 before becoming Labour MP for Shipley in 1935. During his parliamentary career he had been Parliamentary Private Secretary to Ernest Bevin (another Bristolian) from 1940 to 1944, before being promoted to the Colonial Office, first as Parliamentary Under-Secretary and finally as Secretary of State. Apart from his national reputation, he had another attribute which it was felt would enhance his chances of winning the nomination: his brother lived in the constituency and was a Co-operative Insurance Society agent and a local Labour councillor.

Mrs Nichol, too, had a parliamentary background. She had been elected as MP for Bradford North in 1945 and held it until her defeat in the 1950 General Election. Ironically, the Conservative candidate she had beaten was Major John Andrews Benn, a cousin of Tony Wedgwood Benn, and later Sir John, third baronet, who married the daughter of Lord Hankey, the diplomat. To pursue the irony further, Sir John Andrews Benn was chairman of Cincinnati Milling Machines Ltd. Tony Wedgwood Benn was to marry a Cincinnati girl, proposing to her after a whirlwind nine days' courtship when they were both at Oxford.

Tony Wedgwood Benn's father had been an MP, as had been both his grandfathers. So it is little wonder that the House of Commons was in his blood. A photograph of his father hangs in 12 Downing Street, office of the Government Chief Whip, as one of the Liberal Whips in Asquith's 1910 Government. His father had served in the Royal Flying Corps in the First World War and had a most distinguished war record. For most of his parliamentary career he was a Liberal MP, though latterly he was a Labour MP for eight years: firstly for Aberdeen (1928-1931) and then Manchester Gorton (1937-1942). He was Secretary of State for India from 1929 to 1931 and was created a Viscount in 1942 to strengthen Labour representation in the House of Lords. While the peerage was undoubtedly merited after years of notable public service, it was to sow the seeds of what was to become one of the epic constitutional battles of this century.

The father did not accept the Viscountcy lightly. Indeed, before agreeing to the elevation he consulted his eldest son. As he told the House of Lords, at the time of Anthony Wedgwood Benn's battle to renounce his succession to the peerage:

'I had three sons. The eldest boy, Michael, I consulted. He informed me that he intended to obtain Holy Orders, and was not interested in the House of Commons. In any case, the peerage and the priesthood would be a double bar. When he knew, he was as proud as I was about it, and he willingly accepted. The second boy [Tony Wedgwood Benn] was a schoolboy, rather a chatterbox, and I did not consider it necessary to consult him at all. I now wonder very much whether I was right or wrong. But it was difficult, and I did not consult him. I can remember that when the announcement was made in *The Times*, he was very angry and abused me. But in point of fact our minds were on something quite different; and that was the war. Both

14

of these boys were thinking of one thing, and that was how they could manage to get into the Air Force, as volunteers, before they were called up. They both succeeded and became pilots. Unfortunately, and unhappily for me, my eldest son was killed.'

There were, as I said, three candidates before the selection conference that November. Tony Wedgwood Benn, to some people's surprise, was selected on the first ballot. Twenty years later he revealed in the *Bristol Evening Post*, why he thought he had won over the strong candidature of Creech Jones. His account is worth recalling, especially as I believe there are other reasons which he forbore from mentioning. He wrote:

> 'Two factors were working against him. First the Labour selection conference had had a Cabinet Minister (i.e. Cripps) as its MP on and off for 10 years and they were afraid that if they selected Creech Jones he would go straight back into the Cabinet and the constituency would lose the sense of having a Member all to itself.
>
> The second reason was that Transport House (Labour Party headquarters) overdid the pressure. The national agent, Dick Windle, actually came down to the selection conference personally to see that nothing went wrong. Anyone who knew anything about Bristol South-East would have known that was bound to have the very opposite effect.'

I do not think that too much should be made of the presence of the national agent at this selection conference. It is quite usual for national officers of the Labour Party to concern themselves in by-elections. In 1957, at the first Labour constituency meeting to discuss the preparations for a by-election in Bristol West, the national agent, Len Williams, was present. This is particularly easy to remember because when his 'pep talk' was in full flight, the shilling ran out in the electricity meter and the room was plunged into darkness. Chaos reigned until another coin was scrabbled into the meter. Thus the great Labour Party machine in action!

There was something else that Wedgwood Benn wrote in the *Bristol Evening Post* at this time which I found extraordinary. He revealed the voting figures in his selection as the Labour candidate. He wrote: 'I later heard that the first ballot had given Mrs Nichol four votes, Creech Jones 11 and me, 40; and they decided to make it unanimous.' When I first read this I thought it was rather ungallant to reveal the humiliatingly small total of votes scored by Mrs Nichol. After all, she had been a Labour MP, having beaten one of Benn's relatives who was standing as a Conservative for the Bradford seat. But on reflection I thought that perhaps the old adage of blood being thicker than water applied. In any case, it is customary after a selection conference to select the winner unanimously.

There is no doubt that Wedgwood Benn made a magnificent speech at the selection conference. His oratory was already well-developed. He had recently done an extensive university debating tour of the United States together with Edward Boyle, who was to become a Tory Secretary of State for Education, and Kenneth Harris, the writer and journalist, on behalf of Oxford University. Wedgwood Benn's selection conference speech contained local references and had some of the ladies in tears. With his red tie and RAF blue pullover, the impression of vigorous youth was overwhelming.

What Wedgwood Benn did not touch upon in those newspaper articles is how he came to have the nomination for one of Labour's safest seats in the first place. He was at the tender age of 25, not having fought a parliamentary seat. His work experience was extremely limited. He had been, briefly, a salesman for the family publishing firm of Benn Brothers and then a producer on the North American service of the BBC.

It is said that Wedgwood Benn was a protégé of the late Tony Crosland, who was to become a Cabinet Minister. Certainly Crosland had been Wedgwood Benn's tutor at Oxford, thus giving some authority to the paragraph in Susan Crosland's biography of her late husband: 'At the Bristol by-election Tony Benn won the seat, whereupon he made a public announcement that he must lose the stigma of being an intellectual. "You'd better acquire the stigma before worrying about losing it," his former teacher said.'

Certainly at the time, Tony Crosland was the much-loved and respected MP for the immediately neighbouring constituency of South Gloucestershire and would have had good contacts in Bristol South-East. One of these contacts was the Reverend Mervyn Stockwood, later better known as the radical Bishop of Southwark but who, at the time, was the vicar of St Matthew Moorfield in Bristol. Hugh Dalton recorded in his diaries that he had been told in confidence by Tony Crosland that he (Crosland) had worked Wedgwood Benn's successful candidature for Bristol South-East by introducing him to Mervyn Stockwood, a close friend of Sir Stafford Cripps.

Mervyn Stockwood's parish was in the heart of the poorest area of Bristol South-East. He was also a Labour councillor on Bristol City Council struggling against the appalling deprivation in his area. That he pushed hard for Wedgwood Benn's nomination can hardly be doubted. Indeed, there is a revealing anecdote told by a prominent Bristol businessman, George McWatters, a Citizen (i.e. Conservative) city councillor and several times parliamentary candidate. He tells the story of how he was once in a restaurant and was approached by Mervyn Stockwood, who said he would like to introduce him to the next Member of Parliament for Bristol South-East. Standing beside him was Anthony Wedgwood Benn. It was certainly a revelation to McWatters, for he would have known that the Labour selection conference had yet to take place. Mervyn Stockwood's role in promoting the interests of this young Labour nominee makes it all the more difficult to understand why there should be rather unkind references to him in the first volume of Wedgwood Benn's own diaries. In volume two of the diaries Benn also shows a parting of the ways with his former mentor, Tony Crosland.

The by-election itself did not command a great deal of national interest. There were the usual public meetings, the speakers supporting Wedgwood Benn including Barbara Castle, Mervyn Stockwood, Michael Foot and Horace King, who, in the 1960s, was to become a Speaker of the House of Commons. Benn himself went through the normal processes of any parliamentary candidate. During the day he drove himself round with two young men who were his dayshift workers, Leonard Allen and Keith Hooper, both senior boys at Queen Elizabeth's Hospital School, giving out leaflets and knocking on doors. He joked at the time that although he was only 25, his political age was 73 – a reference to his father's age and the succession to the title that hung over him.

There was little in the way of electoral organisation, but this is not a criticism. In those days there was a loyalty among Labour voters that did not waver. It is often forgotten that between 1945-51, Attlee's Government never lost a by-election, a formidable record. Indeed, when Labour lost power in 1951 it did so despite piling up the largest vote that any political party had received in Britain up to that time. The election was lost purely and simply because of the detailed work that the Conservatives put into the organisation of the postal vote in key marginal constituencies. This needs mentioning because the myth survives until this day that the Labour Government was voted out of office solely because of its policies. The fact was that the Tories were better at organising the postal vote than Labour. The part played by the postal vote in the 1951 Conservative victory was confirmed for me by a friend of mine, a university lecturer who from time to time visited Leyhill Open Prison to lecture to the inmates on government and politics. He made this point about the effect of the postal vote and one of the prisoners interrupted to say: 'I can confirm what the lecturer is saying because my agent told me that I won my seat on the postal vote!' Keen students of politics will perhaps need no further clues to identify from whom this contribution came. Sufficient here to say that it was not a former Labour MP who had fallen from grace and was then a guest in one of Her Majesty's penal establishments.

But back to the by-election. It came as a surprise that when Wedgwood Benn published his diaries, *Out of the Wilderness*, he should make rather disparaging references to the lack of organisation in Bristol South-East. In this he misunderstands the nature of the Labour Party at that time. In safe Labour seats there was very little formal organisation at election time. After the 1951 result there was a realisation that more would have to be done, but the concentration was in marginal seats. Safe seats were expected to cooperate with personnel and resources by working with neighbouring marginal seats. Despite this lack of organisation, Bristol South-East consistently turned in good results, both at national and local council level.

One would have thought that Wedgwood Benn would have been aware of this because, although only 25 when he was first elected, it was stated in the local press at the time of his selection that he had been on the Labour Party's list of people prepared to be candidates for three years. Indeed, I was told that he had already turned down approaches to stand in Conservative-held seats.

2

CREDENTIALS

My own involvement with the Labour Party did not begin until January 1955. I had been spending a weekend at Plymouth when I heard a middle-class family running down the railwaymen who were then involved in one of their rare disputes. My mother's father began his working life as a porter on the old Southern Railway. Eventually he was to become a chief inspector at Brighton. I could not equate the nonsense I heard at Plymouth with my memories of my grandfather so I thought if people were talking this sort of claptrap I had to do something about it. So I joined the Labour Party the day I got back to Bristol. The person who signed me up was Beryl Urquhart, a dedicated Labour worker and a former loyal servant of the Parliamentary Labour Party, who is to figure later when we examine one of the most extraordinary speeches that Wedgwood Benn ever made.

I had been brought up in a Labour family. My father was a lifelong supporter of the Party. A Congregational minister, he was at that time principal of Western College, Bristol, a Congregational training college for the ministry. When he had his first church at Winchester, from 1917, he was the only Labour person on the dreaded Board of Guardians. These Boards were the only form of public assistance available. Often applicants had to sell any decent furniture they had before relief would be granted. It was my father who coined the phrase 'The Labour Party owes more to Methodism than to Marx' which was put into popular use by the late Morgan Phillips, a former General Secretary of the Labour Party.

Attending Bristol University on an ex-serviceman's grant, having done two years' National Service in the Royal Navy, I had no inclination towards university politics. Nor was I attracted to the Church, although it was my grandfather Cocks's wish that I follow my father in this respect. I always felt that the attitude of the Church to social issues was 'wishy-washy'. Once in the Labour Party, however, I felt that I could do much more to improve people's conditions both at home and abroad – even if only in a small way.

When I joined the party I lived in the Bristol West constituency, the only safe Conservative seat in Bristol. Realising the hopelessness of the task that faced us there, I suggested that our resources be concentrated in trying to hold the neighbouring Bristol seats. In January 1958, I was chosen as the prospective parliamentary candidate in the West constituency, and immediately encouraged the local party workers to devote their energies elsewhere. Strange though it may seem to some of today's 'hard-left' in Bristol and elsewhere, at that time, I was regarded as one of the most promising left-wingers in Bristol! In the late 1950s I was elected first vice-chairman and then chairman of the Borough Labour Party, the youngest person at the time to have held the post. I used the position to update the party's attitude to electioneering in general. For the first time we produced details of the various council seats and the swings in the votes needed to win marginals. This enabled us to target our efforts more effectively.

In the meantime, the 1959 General Election had been and gone, and so had Labour's chances of being returned to power. There was a national swing against the Party. In Bristol, Labour lost two seats. The result in Bristol West was a thumping Conservative majority of some 20,000! Rather than being grateful for saving my deposit, I even boasted that the result showed a 0.1 per cent swing to Labour against the national trend. It was very much a family election: my sister Doris was my election agent, my brother was a number taker and my parents voted for me. Elections were not bedevilled by opinion polls in those days. They appeared from time to time, but there was not the constant taking of the political temperature that we have nowadays. Nor had the Liberals got fully into their stride with their technique of holding their own straw polls in constituencies to try and produce a bandwagon effect for their candidates. Canvassing was a straightforward business of identifying your supporters and then trying to ensure they voted on the day.

It was a time epitomised by Harold Macmillan's slogan, 'You've never had it so good', but that was not the way many of us saw it in Bristol. Severe damage had been done to Labour in previous years by a combination of council house rent increases and large scale compulsory purchase orders by the Labour-controlled council in the old 'Coronation Street' area of terraced houses in the city heartland.

This early experience of electoral setback at local council level taught me how difficult it is to establish the connection between actions taken by councils and national legislation passed by Parliament. We pointed out, in vain, that slum clearance with absurdly low compensation was ordained from on high. It was impossible to establish the connection in people's minds. I even went so far as to suggest that if, as we were told, the Government would do the clearance if the council refused, then we should do exactly that – refuse. In this way the blame would be laid fairly and squarely on the Government. It was a proposition which led to me being accused of advocating anarchy by some Labour stalwarts.

When I had finished my two years as Bristol Borough Party Chairman, I did less in Bristol politics as I was selected as the prospective parliamentary candidate for the neighbouring seat to the north of Bristol – South Gloucestershire. This was a massive seat, both in terms of area and of a rapidly growing population. New housing estates were sprouting up around the urban fringe of Bristol. There were some thirty local Labour branches or contacts in the constituency. Keeping in touch with these and also breaking new ground meant that one could be continuously on the go. My supporters, thankfully, were a superb bunch of people. One in particular, Ray Bromley, worked in the aero engine works where he was an active trade unionist. He was a great friend and party worker. Without his experience as a motor mechanic my clapped out, old Thames twelve-seater could not have been kept on the road.

The constituency proved to be a great training ground in understanding. The contrasts between the rural and urban areas were vivid, as were the disparities in wealth and amenities. When I was first selected there were still some 1,500 houses which were not on the main drainage and had bucket toilets. One of my earliest propaganda points was that there were houses with bucket lavatories within sight of Berkeley power station – one of the first nuclear Magnox power stations to be built and now being decommissioned.

The largest employer in the area was the aircraft and aero engine complex at Filton and Patchway. This industry was so dependent on public money to fund research and development that it was a constant struggle to rebut the tidal wave of rumours which unsettled people about their job prospects. In particular, the early development of the Concorde project was a fertile source of rumour and counter-rumour. The prototype TSR 2 stainless steel and titanium supersonic fighter was also a source of much speculation and the project was eventually cancelled. Electorally, the aircraft industry was a liability because, when in doubt, the workers always tended to vote Conservative.

For an aspiring politician, it was not always easy to graft together in a branch the old established members and the new-comers from the developing estates. It required tact and an understanding of each other's viewpoints for success. However, it was usually done without aggravation. The newcomers usually respected the contribution that the old established members had made in the past, when the going was much tougher. This is mentioned, because later I refer to comments made by Tony Wedgwood Benn about his Bristol South-East constituency party. It is possible that his early entry into West-minster meant he missed out on this essential part of the political learning process.

In the 1964 General Election I was defeated by 3,714 votes. Fighting the seat again in 1966 I lost by 1,424 votes on an increased electorate of 74,023. In the event, this was not the bad news it seemed at the time for me personally. If I had won that General Election in 1966 I would, on the evidence of what

23

occurred nationally, almost certainly have lost in 1970. Clearly, the wheels of fortune had been turning in my favour.

Throughout my time as candidate in South Gloucestershire I had retained my links with Bristol Labour politics through the Bristol Co-operative Committee. The chairman of the committee at the time was the late councillor Roy Willmott, with whom I had been very friendly for years. He was also vice-chairman of the Bristol South constituency party, and it was Roy Willmott who suggested that I might try for selection in Bristol South when the sitting Labour MP, Will Wilkins, decided to retire. The suggestion, let me add, came not through the friendship but because of his hard-headed reasoning. He held the now unfashionable view that one should work an apprenticeship in politics before getting into Parliament. Fortunately, for me, he considered that my record of service in Bristol, together with three general election contests, had suitably 'blooded' me.

When the selection conference was held I managed to win against four other candidates, one of whom was Walter Johnson, who had fought Bristol West for Labour in 1955 and subsequently became MP for Derby. Another was journalist John Grant, later an Islington MP who moved over to the SDP. When the 1970 General Election was called Labour lost badly in the country, but I was lucky to be elected. My political ambition to be a backbench Labour Member of Parliament had been achieved. I enjoyed my time on the backbenches, earning myself on one occasion, the nickname 'The Boozers' Friend', but not for reasons that may immediately spring to mind! The curious will find an explanation later. In 1973, Bob Mellish, then Labour Chief Whip, asked me to become a junior regional whip with responsibilities for Labour MPs from the South-West, the Home Counties and half of the London constituencies. Living in Bristol, I was within comparatively easy reach of London and so did much of the Friday work when the Commons was sitting, since regular attendance on Fridays presented real difficulties for the Scottish and Northern Labour MPs. It was this that gave me a good working knowledge of the private members' bill procedure. It was to prove invaluable.

I also had a crash course in parliamentary procedure in 1971-72 during the passage of the Conservative Government's highly controversial Industrial Relations legislation. The Government Chief Whip, Francis Pym, had upset Bob Mellish by not telling him that he was going to move a timetable or guillotine motion on the Bill. This was a breach of the normal courtesies with which the 'usual channels' treat each other. I should explain that the relationship between Government and Opposition Whips' Offices is referred to as the 'usual channels'. It is backroom work ensuring the smooth running of the parliamentary machine. Bob Mellish was angry with Francis Pym because of his oversight. In protest, Mellish broke off the 'usual channels' relationship, giving Labour backbenchers a free hand to make life difficult for the Government. I was one of the guerilla squad led by Gerald Kaufman, who was to become an exceptionally diligent Minister, and Jim Wellbeloved that kept the Government ministers and backbenchers on parade into the small hours of the night by debating and voting on legislation which would normally have gone through unopposed.

When Labour formed a Government under Harold Wilson early in 1974, I became a Junior Government Whip. In June the same year I was appointed Pairing Whip when Don Concannon, the MP for Mansfield, became a Minister in the Northern Ireland Office. The Pairing Whip is responsible for the arithmetic of winning votes; in other words, making sure there are enough troops on the ground to defeat the opposing parties in the division lobbies. In April 1976 Jim Callaghan, who became Prime Minister on the resignation of Harold Wilson, asked me to become Chief Whip in succession to Bob Mellish. I was to continue as Chief Whip in Opposition when Labour lost the 1979 election, retiring from the post in autumn 1985. Labour's Chief Whip in Opposition is elected annually, so my colleagues must have had some regard for me as I never lost an election for the Chief's job during this time. I left the Commons in June 1987, having been deselected in my Bristol South seat. Thus, some 14 of my 17 years in the House of Commons were spent in the Labour Whips' Office.

This meant full-time attendance at the Commons from Monday to Friday whenever the Commons was sitting. I make no complaint about this, as I loved the work and felt I was doing something really useful. Nor did my local constituency party object. They fully realised the nature of the task I was fulfilling and that my place was at Westminster. Moreover, it was understood that I could only appear in Bristol at weekends and during the parliamentary recess. This tolerance, however, went when the constituency was taken over by the 'hard-left' and I faced accusations that I was not often present at local mid-week meetings. Some of the 'hard-left' knew why I was not present and could have explained to others. For their own reasons they chose to keep silent. This full-time attendance at the Commons was only following the pattern of my predecessor, Will Wilkins, who had been a Whip in the Attlee Government, and had proved himself to be loyal to the core and completely devoted to the Labour movement. But this was ignored. In due time my zealous attendance at the Commons and voting record was turned against me in the move to dislodge me from my seat.

I don't want to turn this into an embryonic autobiography. That is not the purpose. But I would like to mention that during my time as MP I fought a number of campaigns in Parliament on behalf of my constituents and Bristol as a whole. The rentcharge racket, known in the trade as the 'builders' pension fund', was one of them. Together with my friend, the late Fred Evans, formerly Labour MP for Caerphilly, we steered through a private members' bill which prohibited the creation of new rent charges. This was a system of land tenure peculiar to Bristol and Manchester where annual rent charges were imposed on freehold land.

Probably the most popular struggle was with Courage's brewery, and herein lies the story of 'The Boozers' Friend'. When I was first elected in 1970, 47 out of 50 pubs in Bristol South were Courage houses. Not content with this near monopoly, Courage tried to get rid of the cheap pint of ordinary bitter and substitute a more expensive beer called 'Full Brew'. They even had the cheek to advertise this as 'The Regular's Bitter'. At the time I was serving on the standing committee considering the Bill introduced by Ted Heath's Government to denationalise the State pubs in Carlisle and Gretna Green. I used the opportunity to conduct a full frontal attack on Courage, and finally I won. 'Full Brew' disappeared.

Today there is a wide choice of beers in Bristol South. The monopoly has been broken. It was this episode that earned me the nickname. Not, I thought, a bad foundation on which to start building up electoral support!

3

BENN AS BACKBENCHER

The new backbencher Anthony Wedgwood Benn took his seat in the House of Commons on 30 November 1950. Two months later, on 7 February, he made his maiden speech in a debate on the Iron and Steel Industry. After expressing the traditional diffidence expected of a maiden speaker, he gave a well-structured speech, all seventeen minutes of it, in which he included the customary reference to his predecessor, Sir Stafford Cripps. It is also traditional for the next speaker to congratulate the maiden speaker. On this occasion the task fell to Sir Ralph Glyn, Conservative MP for Abingdon. It was no cursory performance, the obligatory tossing off of a few well-chosen remarks before making his own contribution to the debate:

> 'On this occasion I should like to couple the Socialist Party with my congratulations on having obtained an extremely helpful and forceful recruit. Another reason why I am so glad that it falls to me to be able to congratulate the hon. Member is that I am old enough to have sat in the House for a good many years with his father. It makes me feel uncommonly old to see the hon. Member sitting on the benches opposite looking as his father did then, and, indeed as his father does now . . . it is all the more refreshing to have such sane remarks from a Socialist point of view and made by so young a Member of Parliament. We are given great hopes for the future.'

This physical likeness to his father was not the only similarity between the two. In their respective contributions to Lords and Commons affairs they shared identical interests. Both of them concentrated their activities on Foreign, Commonwealth and Colonial matters. The arrival of Wedgwood Benn stimulated a burst of activity by his father. Sometimes these topics were spoken on or asked about almost contemporaneously in both the Lords and the Commons by father and son. Benn's line of questioning as a backbencher is worth closer examination. In the first five years, out of a total of 133 questions, 65 were on the subject of the Colonies, 17 on Foreign Affairs and four were on Commonwealth Relations. In other words, more than half of his written questions were to these three kindred departments. In addition, there were 20 questions to the Home Office, eight of which related to matters regarding aliens. Turning to oral questions during the same period, out of a total of 72 questions, 15 were on the Colonies, eight on Commonwealth Relations and seven on Foreign Affairs. Shown diagramatically this concentration on a few departments stands out dramatically.* Over this period only a handful of questions were asked about Bristol itself. This same concentration can be found in the questions he asked during the period 1956 to 1959. Out of a total of 122 written questions, for example, 62 were asked on the Colonies, 25 on Foreign Affairs and three on Commonwealth Relations. In other words, three quarters of his written questions were directed towards these three departments. As for his 54 oral questions during the same period, 24 were to Foreign Affairs, 18 to the Colonies and one to Commonwealth Relations.

Why was there this great interest and accord with his father? Part of the reason must lie in the fact that between 1929 and 1931, Viscount Stansgate had been Secretary of State for India, while his son, Anthony, was one of the earliest members of the Movement for Colonial Freedom. One can imagine innumerable family conversations when these matters must have been mulled over, and possible opportunities of raising them in both Houses of Parliament discussed.

But there were other issues. A month after his maiden speech, Wedgwood Benn raised the question of conscientious objectors

* See illustration section.

who were prepared to serve a term of imprisonment rather than undertake National Service. This situation would have been familiar to him because of his mother's strong Nonconformist background. Benn was recognising here the over-riding part that conscience can play in decisions of this kind. Yet years later, in the late 1970s and 1980s, he acquiesced in Labour Party annual conference resolutions condemning Labour MPs who invoked the conscience clause over the highly-charged issue of abortion. This was at a time when there was controversy over successive bills to limit abortion. There was also more to this acquiescence by Benn. By not taking up a stance he was supporting Labour conference which thought that by passing a resolution it could order MPs to support Labour Party policy on abortion. This serious erosion of the Nonconformist influence within the Labour Party has done much to narrow its appeal, while also risking the alienation of others, such as Roman Catholics.

In those early days as a backbencher Benn proved himself more realistic about world affairs and the military situation that Britain and her allies faced. In November 1951, in a foreign affairs debate, he acknowledged that the danger of military attack existed. Three years later he told the Commons: ' . . . this last year has been the end of an era, which began in 1947 when the implacable hostility of the Soviet Union became apparent in the West. To me, the Geneva Conference brought to an end an era of fighting between the two sides and the final consolidation of the West. The London-Paris agreements marked the end of that era of the Cold War, and we have now come to the stalemate.'

Throughout this period there were the usual questions on subjects mentioned before. His interest in African affairs was to lead to a major parliamentary coup on 21 March 1952 when he successfully applied for an emergency debate on the question of Seretse Khama and the Chieftainship of the Bamangwato tribe in Bechuanaland. Seretse Khama had been deposed as Chief-Designate of the Bamangwato. Benn's speech, in the view of Fenner Brockway, the veteran colonial affairs campaigner, who seconded the emergency motion, had made him 'a worthy son of his father'. Lord Stansgate, he said, was still standing for the ideals of liberty in the House of Lords, and 'as one of the older

Members of this House, I very sincerely congratulate his son upon that speech and say . . . he expressed all the very best – and that is very great – in the record of his father.'

It was a moving tribute. Ten days after the emergency debate Wedgwood Benn, formerly with the North American service*, was rallying to the side of the BBC in an Opposition debate on Information Services. It is worth quoting this fairly fully in view of later developments in his thinking:

> 'The entire fabric of radio propaganda is built round the news bulletin. It is so in Europe, it is so in our broadcasts to North America and to Latin America. Wherever one goes throughout the world, it is the BBC news bulletin which gives the Corporation its reputation. The reason for this is that the BBC is scrupulously careful to see that its news bulletins are accurate, and that nothing is put in which has not been checked and twice checked. That is why, during the war, the broadcasts to Europe were of such value to people there – they knew that if they heard it on the BBC it was true. So the first essential of radio propaganda is the truth, even when it reacts, as it sometimes does, unfavourably to one's own cause. I do not think that co-ordination between western nations would ever arrive at a better version of truth in news form. At the same time the BBC overseas services follow the principle of the BBC home services – the BBC has no editorial opinion of its own.'

Two years later, in May 1954, he returned to the question of broadcasting in the context of party political broadcasts. He made a strong plea for the choice of political speakers to be left to the Party Whips to nominate. The arrangements for party political broadcasts have always been arranged through contact between the various Whips' offices in the Commons and the broadcasting authorities. The number and length of broadcasts for each individual political party vary according to the number of MPs they have in the Commons and the number of votes cast for each party in the previous general election. Inevitably, there are disagreements, but it is rare for them to surface publicly.

* Benn left his mark on the BBC World Service, accidentally setting fire to a bin of wax swarf and gutting a studio.

As far as the Labour Party was concerned, tensions gradually increased between the leadership of the Parliamentary Party and the Labour Party's National Executive Committee, the body elected by the annual conference to act as custodian of party policy. The issue of broadcasting became one of the manifestations of lack of trust in the parliamentary leadership by certain members of the National Executive. Benn himself was one who wanted to wrest control from the Parliamentary Party's leaders' hands.

During my time as Chief Whip I used to attend the meetings where the allocation of party broadcasts was decided each year. One issue which cropped up during this time was the question of party political broadcasts going out on all television channels simultaneously. For some time I defended the status quo on behalf of the Labour Party. I would counter arguments of the broadcasters to break up simultaneity by asking how they reconciled their views with the continuing simultaneity of the Queen's broadcast to the nation on Christmas Day. I asked them if they had made any approaches to Buckingham Palace to change this practice.

Eventually the pressure became so strong that I had to concede – particularly as the other political parties were prepared to go along with the change. When the National Executive discussed this Wedgwood Benn denounced me vehemently in such terms that I felt that Quisling, Blunt or Burgess were patriotic pillars compared with my supposed treachery. I had been defending the position for the Labour Party. Personally, in point of fact, I had always felt that if a party's broadcasts were so lacking in appeal that the only way that people could be made to watch them was having them on all channels at once – then they were probably doing more harm than good.

Present-day feminists and women's rights campaigners would not like the question put down by Wedgwood Benn in June 1955. He asked the Home Office to draw up electoral registers with the appropriate style Mr, Mrs, or Miss in each case after the names of the registered voters. Actually, this question is a little unworldly because such a course would lead to either the revelation of a number of relationships between unmarried people or the incorrect filling in of the electoral form – which is an offence! Moreover, in these days, unfortunately, it would also provide information for zealous criminals who now comb through electoral registers looking for easy victims for break-ins.

On the other hand, Benn showed great awareness in raising, in February 1956, the question of family allowance books being used as security for loans. Thirty years later, this is still a major problem, coupled as it is with the growth of loan sharks charging exorbitant rates of interest and using very dubious methods of collection.

The year 1956 was the year of the Suez Crisis. Benn was active both inside and outside the House of Commons. Indeed, the Suez affair aroused widespread and spontaneous demonstrations of protest and indignation throughout the Labour and trade union movement. On 5 November that year Benn presented a petition to the Commons asking for the Government to comply with all the resolutions of the United Nations, creating by his action noisy scenes from the Conservative benches. He also spoke on the question of police action towards demonstrators attempting to approach the Palace of Westminster at this time. Following Suez, Wedgwood Benn then questioned the role of the Central Office of Information during the crisis. In particular, he questioned the editorial balance of the material which had been published by the Central Office of Information as being representative of newspaper comment.

There was one other contribution, which is relevant today as we observe his progression from the backbenches through various ministerial appointments. In June 1956 he initiated a major debate on Public Authorities (Public Relations) and called for a Commission of Inquiry 'to study the relationship now existing between these public authorities and private individuals . . . ' As he developed his theme he touched on the role of the MP and the risk of Members of Parliament getting out of touch with the consumers of the services provided by the public authorities of various kinds. Warming to his theme, he then said:

'I believe that my own party, the Labour Party, suffers from a delusion in this matter, a delusion which runs like this, that because the Labour movement sprang from the people, as it manifestly did, it can never really get out of touch with the people. I suggest to the House that whether one's origins were poor or whether they were of the silver spoon in the mouth sort, as soon as one touches and controls the apparatus of the State, then, by that very fact, one is out of touch with ordinary people in the community. Therefore I hope that my own party – and I am sure it will – in the future pays great attention to this problem.'

It was a speech that demonstrated the characteristic thoroughness and originality with which he tackled subjects. But it also indicated something else which only time was to reveal. Having accused the Labour Party of falling into the trap of losing touch with the people and thus shown an awareness of its existence, he was to walk into the trap himself, with near-fatal consequences for the Party he sought to warn.

Benn's period as a backbencher was one of great contrasts. Sometimes there were matters of great principle, others were trivial. He was to resign as a junior Opposition spokesman on the RAF over the question of nuclear weapons. And yet on other occasions he seemed to be ambivalent about his direction and purpose. I quote from an interesting article which appeared in *The Times* on 19 November, 1954. It reported the results of the annual elections for the Parliamentary Party Shadow Cabinet. Benn was one of the unsuccessful candidates and the following correction appears at the end of the article: 'Mr Wedgwood Benn was inaccurately described earlier this week as being among the Bevanite candidates. It appears that he should more correctly be described as being on the Right wing of the middle-of-the-roaders, with a strong radical bias.' It was an equivocation that makes the Vicar of Bray looked like a rolled steel joist.

In the speech quoted earlier, Wedgwood Benn referred to the origins of 'silver spoon in the mouth'. Perhaps this applied to him. Not in the sense of an aristocratic background nor inherited wealth; rather in having an abundance of vicarious political experience and expertise on hand through his father right from the start. Because of this he may well have short-circuited some of the essential learning processes that ordinary backbenchers have to go through when they arrive at the House of Commons. Certainly, this would account for some of the weaknesses he was to show later.

4

OPPOSITION SPOKESMAN 1957-64

Early in 1957 Anthony Wedgwood Benn received his first front bench appointment, as Opposition spokesman for the Royal Air Force. This must have pleased him in view of the family association with this Service and his father's distinguished war record. His first speech from the front bench was during the annual debate on the Air Estimates. In it he referred to the arrival of the atomic bomb and the V-bomber creating an atomic stalemate. He went on: 'Our policy is based on this deadlock in co-existence and our defence policy is based on it.' The point was reinforced later when he said, 'Time and again in the House the Prime Minister has said: in effect, in answer to questions – it has been said by others, and is in general, agreed by the Opposition – that if the hydrogen bomb exists, this country must have it.'

This was at a time when the Campaign for Nuclear Disarmament (CND) was going strong. The Aldermaston marches were well-established as annual features of the campaigning for unilateralism. There was a perfectly respectable case to be made out for the policy at this stage. Apart from the superpowers of the United States and Soviet Union, Britain was the only country with atomic weapons. For Britain to surrender its weapons as part of a global package to stop the proliferation of nuclear weapons to other countries made a great deal of sense intellectually. The great danger in most people's minds has always been that nuclear weapons would be used in some war between two other countries. This would have the effect of sucking the two major superpowers into the maelstrom. In my experience, before CND declined in the 1960s, there was a change in public mood. When CND began, people wanted Britain to keep nuclear weapons regardless of what other countries did. By the time CND waned, people, generally, were prepared to surrender our nuclear weapons as part of a general disarmament package.

Wedgwood Benn, on 29 July 1957, initiated a major debate on a ruling by the Speaker which turned down an application for an emergency debate on Muscat and Oman. Wedgwood Benn tabled a motion questioning this decision and during the course of his remarks he discoursed on the party system. They are worth repeating if only to record what he thought then and what he subsequently came to believe:

> 'The party system is well embedded in our form of Parliamentary Government. We all know that one cannot get elected to Parliament unless one has a party label. We know when we come here that the organisation of business is done through the Whips. I think that I am a good party man. I believe that we can achieve nothing unless we act together and I also believe that we must be prepared to hang together . . . But I accept the Party. For the modern party system, even at its most oppressive, does not in any way limit our right to speak. It may limit how we vote at the end of the day, although in my own party and in the party opposite me we have the right of abstention on grounds of principle. That is a comfort which I draw from the restriction of the party system.'

It was a further reaffirmation of the right of a Member of Parliament to exercise his conscience. Certainly as far as the Labour, Liberal and Conservative Parties are concerned, issues such as capital punishment, abortion, homosexuality and licensing laws have always been regarded as matters of conscience. But it is a right which sometimes can be abused. When Ernest Bevin was Foreign Secretary he once received a delegation from a group of Labour backbenchers who were opposed to the then

Government policy of German re-armament. He listened to them patiently as each said he wanted to exercise his right of conscience and oppose the Government. As they were leaving his room he called them back and said he now knew the collective noun for those who exercised the right of conscience to dissent. 'It's called a conspiracy,' he said and bid them good night. During my time as Labour Chief Whip, trying to sustain a minority Government, I had to be fairly robust with some of my colleagues who tried to extend the conscience provision to excuse themselves from supporting some aspects of the Government's general policy. Fortunately, I was able to stamp out this malaise before it got a hold. Otherwise, the Government would have fallen in a matter of weeks.

Wedgwood Benn went on to say that it was difficult for back-benchers to find opportunities to raise matters in the Commons Chamber. 'We have to grub for our food,' he complained. By this he meant that 'A Parliamentary Question is all that we get, and it is a job very often to get the chance to ask a supplementary.' The hope of backbenchers was that they would get the evening adjournment. In fact, during this period of time he did not grub particularly effectively. His contributions in the House on Air Force matters were rather sparse. In the event, as we have noted, he was to resign this post on the question of nuclear weapons.

Possibly he was more preoccupied with getting himself known in the Labour Party throughout the country, for in 1959 he was elected to the National Executive. At this time, the practice whereby some Labour MPs use the Commons Chamber to obtain self-publicity in the summer months had not begun. It is not uncommon these days because the local Labour parties meet during this time to decide who to vote for in the National Executive elections. Some MPs even create scenes and get themselves ejected from the Commons in the hope of squeezing out extra sympathy votes from the local parties who do not understand the very sophisticated House of Commons system. The advent of radio broadcasting of Parliament has encouraged this practice.

Wedgwood Benn was also extremely active in the Fabian Society, the long-established discussion group founded by

Sidney and Beatrice Webb, Bernard Shaw and others. He was to become its chairman and wrote pamphlets, including one on the House of Lords. But more of this later.

On 31 January 1958, Wedgwood Benn was back to protesting about the backbenchers' lot. He complained of the lack of facilities for Members, particularly in undertaking the welfare aspects of their jobs. He raised the question of the privileges of Privy Councillors, who have a right to preference when speakers are called in debates, and the question of committee work. Later on, when Wedgwood Benn himself was a Privy Councillor, I do not recall him ever attempting or representing that he should forego this privilege. As for committee work, he returned to the theme in a debate on the Life Peerages Bill a month later:

> 'Do not let us make the mistake of thinking that distinguished men will do the donkey work. They will not. We know from this House and from our party in this House that the donkey work is not done by the people who are likely candidates for life peerages. The donkey work in Committee is done by the people who are willing to regard Parliament and Parliamentary work as their first call.'

Looking at Wedgwood Benn's own record of committee work during his time in the House of Commons, one is led to wonder how he categorises himself. The real 'donkey work' he alluded to is done in the Standing Committees which undertake detailed examination of Bills. This is the detailed scrutiny often referred to as 'line by line, clause by clause'. In view of his comments it is not inappropriate to draw attention to Benn's own devotion to the so-called donkey work. How does his record stand? Examination of the record suggests not very highly. From the time he entered the House of Commons in 1950 until the end of the session 1986-87, the record shows that out of a possible attendance of 116 committee meetings, Wedgwood Benn attended 73 times – and 42 of these were as a Minister responsible for departmental Bills which were being examined. As a means of putting his attendance record in context, during the session 1971-72, I was summoned by the clerks of the committee to be present on 77 occasions and attended 76 times.

In the background of his activities, of course, there was the personal dilemma which needed resolving. His father's peerage, which had been conferred upon him before life peers were introduced, was an hereditary title. On his father's death, Anthony Wedgwood Benn would succeed to the title and thus be disqualified from membership of the House of Commons. He began taking evasive action by presenting his Parliament Bill on 12 January 1958. Essentially this was a propaganda exercise. Its stated purpose was: 'To alter the composition of the House of Lords by removing its hereditary basis; to reduce its powers and to increase the powers of the House of Commons . . . ' Time was to show that of the eleven sponsors of the Bill, no fewer than five were to become life peers themselves.

A month later, in February 1958, he was speaking in another debate, this time on the second reading of the Life Peerages Bill. Although another MP in the debate, Robin Cooke, the Conservative Member for Bristol West, had referred to Wedgwood Benn's own particular difficulty, Benn correctly pointed out that the Bill had nothing to do with heirs to peerages. 'The view I take on this point, which I stick to and which I believe is right, is that this (Bill) has nothing to do with House of Lords reform,' he said. 'I am a Member of the House of Commons and I do not believe that peers should be allowed to sit here, even if they renounce their rights.'

But he also said something else, a viewpoint which was to resurface years later in more dramatic circumstances: 'Let us not make any mistake about it,' he began. 'When the Leader of the House said that there was no upper limit to this process he was creating for us a weapon which I hope a future Labour Prime Minister will be ready to use. I have the right hon. Gentleman's words in my mind now . . . He said, "We think the discretion of a Prime Minister ought to be sufficient to decide how many life peers should be created. The weapon of swamping the House of Lords with life peers, if ever it has to be done, will be in the hands of a Labour Prime Minister. It is too late for the Bill to be dropped, but in the future, if ever we should need to use the power we shall do so . . . " '

This idea of swamping the House of Lords was used by Benn to great effect at subsequent Labour Party conferences during the 1980s. Party conferences are not just about the set-piece debates in the hall; there are also 'fringe meetings' held by subject interest groups wanting to draw attention to their campaigns. Left-wing activist groups are not slow in seizing the opportunity and Benn was invited to speak at many of them. This was when he was busy generating the head of steam needed to bulldoze through major constitutional changes. Yet he was not being completely frank about the proposition. Apart from anything else, the procedures of the Lords are such that only a maximum of four new peers can be introduced in any week when the Lords is sitting. Moreover, the House of Lords would be unlikely to modify its procedures at a time when it was faced with the threat of being 'swamped'.

There is a gap between Wedgwood Benn's thinking and reality. How large can be judged by his rhetoric at one party conference when he told delegates that a Labour Government should create a thousand peers to overcome any stonewalling by the House of Lords. That would have taken 250 weeks of the Lords' time at least to implement. In other words, about eight years, or two full parliamentary terms. How a Labour Government would get through its other legislation in the meantime he did not venture to outline. None the less, the 'swamping' line was extremely popular with active party members. Wedgwood Benn would go into a 'fringe' meeting at conference and say, in his introductory remarks, that he was collecting names for a thousand peers who were going to abolish the Lords. He would then call for 'volunteers'. The reluctant peer had become a rhetorical recruiting sergeant!

But all this was in the future. In the committee stage of the Life Peerages Bill he said: 'It is laughable to suggest that these life peers are intended to work in the House of Lords. There is no evidence of that. The only people who do work there are the superannuated members of the House of Commons who do so out of nostalgia. They record their votes in much the same way as they have done during a long period of service in the House of Commons.' Subsequent events were to show that he was very wide of the mark. In any case, his reference to former colleagues who were now in the House of Lords did not show him at his most kindly.

One other remark from these proceedings is interesting: 'I am an abolitionist (of the House of Lords), but not a unicameralist, but I think that the unicameralists should now present their view not as an ideal, but as a practical way forward.' What he was saying was that although he was in favour of the abolition of the House of Lords, he did not believe in a single chamber government. There was a need for a second chamber of some sort apart from the House of Commons. It was not a view that he sustained. Later he was saying frequently that a second chamber was not necessary.

The 1959 General Election defeat was a grave setback for Labour. Soon afterwards the policy of unilateral disarmament became a dominant issue within the Party leading to titanic clashes at the annual party conference. It was a policy that was adopted by the Labour conference at Scarborough in 1960. It was at this conference that Anthony Wedgwood Benn went to see Hugh Gaitskell to suggest a compromise on the issue. He emerged whitefaced saying, 'He called me Judas Iscariot.'

When the House of Commons returned after the general election, Gaitskell, previous biblical references notwithstanding, soon appointed Wedgwood Benn, to the front bench as spokesman on Transport matters. His appointment, in fact, reflected his election by the Parliamentary Party to Labour's Shadow Cabinet. He had tried previously to be elected but without success. This Shadow Cabinet position, together with his membership of the National Executive, meant that, in terms of stature within the Parliamentary Party and the Labour movement in the country, Benn had definitely 'arrived'. To what use he was to put this elevation we shall see in due course.

Though he was spokesman on Transport, this did not prohibit him from speaking on other subjects. One contribution is of especial interest. During a debate on accommodation in the House of Commons, in March 1960, he made the following observation:

'The power of the modern pressure groups in this country

is increasingly being achieved by persuasion. People do not any longer use the big stick to get their way. They employ the public relations officer and the research agencies. Like every hon. Member, I am bombarded with statistics and glossy publications designed to convince me that I want to adopt a particular attitude towards the road lobby, towards the licensed trade or this or that. I do not object to them bringing pressure or seeking to bring pressure on me because that is their job as the pressure group. But it is my job to have the equipment behind me to assess whether their claims are just, whether their figures are accurate, and whether what they ask is in the public interest.'

These comments on pressure groups were fair. The position today, twenty-five years after he made the comments, is very much worse. The current trend is becoming more and more akin to the sort of lobbying that goes on in the United States. The pity, however, is that he did not show the same appreciation of the way in which particular pressure groups have latched onto and exploited the Labour Party itself. They are using the Party as a ready-made vehicle to propagate their own particular points of view. There has to be an explanation for this contradiction. Perhaps it is that he was too eager to use these groups for his own purposes.

Benn used his position as Labour's Transport spokesman effectively. He raised specific issues, such as traffic congestion, parking and road casualties. In the course of one speech he advocated that the question of the compulsory wearing of seat belts in cars should be considered. It was another twenty years before such a measure became law. In another speech he made the case for an integrated transport system, probably one of the first occasions that the concept, which was to become a hoary old Labour slogan, raised its head.

At the opening of the new session of Parliament in November 1960, Benn made a substantial speech on foreign affairs. It was a *tour d'horizon*, showing great breadth of thinking. It was, in a way, almost a swan song. Though he raised other issues during that month, this speech was to be his last major contribution in the House of Commons for nearly three years. His father,

43

LABOUR AND THE BENN FACTOR

Viscount Stansgate died on 17 November and Wedgwood Benn succeeded to his title. The long constitutional struggle to renounce his prospective peerage, which had hung over his parliamentary career, now began in earnest.

5

HOUSE OF LORDS: PEERAGE

Describing in his diaries how Wedgwood Benn got the selection in Bristol South-East, Hugh Dalton said that Benn wanted some years in the Commons before going to the Lords. However, elected in 1950 as the youngest MP, it soon became clear that Benn was determined not to be denied a career in the House of Commons because of the vagaries of the hereditary system. It was not long before moves were made to clear this legal impediment.

As early as 1953 Reggie Paget, Labour MP for Northampton, had presented a Ten Minute Rule Bill in the Commons which would have allowed MPs inheriting titles to be exempt if they so wished. Paget was something of a character, not an entirely typical Labour MP as he used to go fox hunting regularly. Ten Minute Rule Bills rarely succeed in becoming law unless there is not only support from all parties but also virtually no opposition. In reality, they are a method of drawing attention to an issue. Paget was merely using the occasion for publicity since a major constitutional issue like this clearly could not be decided in this way.

In his speech, Reggie Paget cited the case of the MP for South Dorset (Viscount Hinchingbrooke), who was in the same position as Wedgwood Benn. Paget declared: 'So long as the electors of Dorset South are deluded enough to elect him, it is unfair that they should be deprived of his services.' He added, 'I say equally, that it is unfair on the electors of Bristol South-East, so long as they are wise enough to elect their present Member, that they should be deprived of his services.'

This theme was to recur time and again throughout Wedgwood Benn's campaign. It was a sentiment with which few could disagree. It was all the more strange, therefore, that years later Benn, with his customary zeal, was to throw himself into the campaign for mandatory reselection of sitting Labour MPs. This is the process which has removed from Parliament a number of Labour MPs in whom the electorate has repeatedly shown confidence by voting them back to Parliament at election after election.

In November 1954 Wedgwood Benn drafted the Stansgate Titles Deprivation Bill. It was based on the Titles Deprivation Act of 1917, which was perhaps not the most fortunate precedent since this Act was passed to 'deprive Enemy Peers and Princes of British Dignities and Titles'. It stated that 'a person shall be deemed to have adhered to His Majesty's enemies if since the commencement of the present war he has voluntarily resided in an enemy country or if he has served in the enemy forces or in any way rendered assistance to the enemy.' Anti-German feelings ran high in the First World War and showed themselves in irrational ways. People would kick German dachshund or 'sausage' dogs in the street and break the windows of shops with German-sounding names over them. It was at this time that the Royal Family changed its name from Wettin to Windsor and the Battenberg family became Mountbatten.

Clearly, the Stansgate Titles Deprivation Bill was an unsuitable vehicle for Wedgwood Benn's purposes, but I suppose he thought it was a further chance to ventilate the issue. It made little progress, being referred to the House of Lords as a Personal rather than a Public Bill. A month later, December 1954, Wedgwood Benn presented a petition to the Lords, the object of which was to allow him to denounce his succession to the Viscountcy of Stansgate. The Bill itself was turned down by the Lords because it was regarded as raising 'questions of general importance'. It was not proper, as a Personal Bill, to have the authority to alter a matter of such constitutional importance.

The following year, in March 1955, his father, Lord Stansgate, rectifying the previous deficiencies, introduced a Public Bill into the Lords entitled the Wedgwood Benn (Renunciation) Bill. A major debate took place on 26 April. Viscount Stansgate outlined the work of a modern MP, stressing that this particular case was unrelated to the general subject of House of Lords reform. Winding up his speech in grand style he quoted from a letter sent by Winston Churchill to his son, Anthony, some two weeks earlier. Churchill had written: 'As I wrote to you confidentially in September 1953, I certainly feel yours is a very hard case, and I am personally strongly in favour of sons having the right to renounce irrevocably the peerages they inherit from their fathers. This would not, of course, prevent them from accepting another peerage, if they were offered one, later on.'

At the end of the debate twenty-four peers voted in favour of the Bill and fifty-two voted against.

The next stage was in the House of Commons on 29 April 1955. Wedgwood Benn presented a petition relating to the Viscountcy of Stansgate. He said it was from the Lord Mayor, Aldermen and Burgesses of Bristol. It outlined the problem that on the death of his father the city would be deprived of one of its MPs. He finished by quoting the concluding words that Anthony Neil Wedgwood Benn . . . 'may be enabled to continue to serve Her Majesty's Loyal Subjects the Burgesses of Bristol as a Commoner in the Commons House of Parliament so long as he may be elected as one of their representatives according to law.'

While I would not want to shatter any cherished illusions, it must be said that presenting petitions to Parliament is of limited use in terms of getting anything done. A petition is ordered to 'lie upon the Table' and nothing further is done in terms of House of Commons action. In other words, like the Ten Minute Rule Bill, it is a propaganda exercise to keep the issue before the public eye.

On 17 November 1960 Lord Stansgate died suddenly. When the news broke in Bristol, speculation immediately arose about the by-election and a possible successor to Wedgwood Benn. The chairman of the Bristol South-East Labour Party,

Councillor Bert Peglar, paid tribute to Benn's excellent service as MP and went on to say: 'We realised that we should have to lose him to the other House eventually.' He also went on to state that he had a 'completely open mind' on the question of a successor.

Everybody, however, had reckoned without the tenacity of Wedgwood Benn. Another petition was presented to the House of Commons, this time for the appointment of a Select Committee to deal with Benn's problem: namely that he was now a Member of Parliament and a Peer. An illegal combination. The matter was referred to the Committee of Privileges, which could find no support for the proposition that one man is legally entitled to be a Member of both Houses simultaneously. The Committee concluded that Wedgwood Benn was disqualified from membership of the House of Commons on his succession to the Viscountcy of Stansgate. Benn in the meantime, however, had persuaded his local party to support him. All talk of his successor, therefore, was shelved indefinitely. There were a few grumbles, but by and large he had solid backing.

On 23 March 1961 the campaign entered another phase. Sir Lynn Ungoed-Thomas, Labour's legal spokesman in the Commons, introduced the Peerages Renunciation Bill. It was the forerunner of the Life Peerages Act of 1963 which finally gave Wedgwood Benn what he wanted. There was also another petition, this time presented by Will Wilkins, Benn's neighbouring Labour MP in Bristol South. It was signed by 10,357 electors in his South-East constituency. It stated that Benn 'who has been four times returned to Parliament as the Member for the said constituency of Bristol South-East, now stands in immediate danger of disqualification solely because of an inheritance for which he is not responsible and which he wishes to renounce.'

Meanwhile, there was activity of a different kind. Labour's Charlie Pannell (Leeds West), an old hand at parliamentary procedure, pressed the Speaker about the possibility of Wedgwood Benn addressing the House of Commons from the Bar of the House. This is the area facing the Speaker between the two sides of the Chamber, but outside the technical limits of the

'House' itself. The Speaker ruled that unless the House of Commons decided otherwise Benn could not come to speak.

Wedgwood Benn, undaunted, wrote to the Speaker asking to be allowed to be admitted to speak on the report from the Committee of Privileges. Lending support was Hugh Gaitskell, who, as Leader of the Opposition, moved that 'Mr Anthony Wedgwood Benn be admitted in and heard.' It led to a full-scale debate, a formidable list of speakers voicing the different sides of the argument. But when the motion was put to the vote it was lost by 152 to 221 – a majority against of 69. Benn would not be permitted to speak. The next step was the debate on the Privileges Committee report itself. Again there was a notable array of speakers from both sides. When the vote came to approve the recommendation of the Privileges Committee – that is, that Benn should be disqualified as a Member – the motion was carried by 204 to 126 – a majority of 78. It was a clear cut decision and meant 'curtains' for Wedgwood Benn, unless the law was changed. On 18 April 1961, the writ for a by-election in Bristol South-East was issued.

It would be idle to pretend that there was complete unanimity in the Bristol South-East Labour Party about fielding a candidate in the by-election who might not be allowed to take his seat if elected. Some wanted an unencumbered candidate. Indeed this feeling was shared by some at the Labour Party national headquarters at Transport House. I have been told that it was only by one vote that a sub-committee of Labour's National Executive decided to let Wedgwood Benn run without an official Labour candidate in the field against him. Benn, therefore, became Labour's standard bearer.

At this time, I was chairman of the Bristol Borough Labour Party. One evening I went to Bristol South-East to do some canvassing and called at the house of Tom Martin, a long-standing city councillor for a ward in the South-East constituency. He seemed totally nonplussed by my request for canvassing material to start work. Rather than giving me the material he referred me to Ted Bishop, another city councillor. His attitude puzzled me. However, having since read the references to Tom Martin in Benn's diary *Out of the Wilderness*, the response has become more understandable.

49

Benn described him as being hostile to the peerage campaign throughout and a troublemaker.

Ted Bishop was much more helpful, supplying me with an electoral register to work from. This was the first of a number of canvasses I did during the by-election campaign. Canvassing, normally, is a chore. On this occasion, however, it was different. The level of awareness as to the reason for the by-election was high. Most people were sympathetic over the constitutional issue involved. Labour supporters were solidly in support as one would expect; but there was also a great deal of support from Conservatives and Liberals. Many Conservatives said they would vote for Wedgwood Benn purely on the constitutional issue. Naturally, it would be entirely without prejudice to their normal political beliefs! Others, of course, were immovable. I felt sorry for one elderly lady who said she couldn't support Mr Wedgwood Benn, although she sympathised with him, because her husband had made her promise never to vote Labour when he was on his death bed.

The constituency was not well organised, as Wedgwood Benn himself admits, but frankly it was not necessary, as I pointed out when dealing with the 1950 by-election. The great drive in both major political parties at this time was to concentrate on marginal seats which were likely to change hands. Bristol South-East did not come into this category. The most memorable meeting was at Chiphouse School in Kingswood when I had to speak before Michael Foot. As I spoke I could read the thoughts of the audience quite clearly: When is this earnest young man going to shut up and sit down so that we can hear Michael Foot? It was at this meeting that Wedgwood Benn ran into real trouble with a questioner who asked him why he had his children educated privately. Benn's reply, as recorded in the *Bristol Evening Post*, was that his children 'had been sent to public school because education was "something that is bought" and that Eton, for instance, had a reputation because the investment per child was infinitely higher than that obtained under the State system.'

This was the only time I ever saw or heard of him being in any difficulty throughout the campaign, which attracted many well-known figures in his support right across the spectrum of the

Party: Harold Wilson, Donald Soper, Charlie Pannell, Philip Hopkins, Jo Grimond, Tony Crosland, Fenner Brockway, James Cameron, Malcolm Muggeridge, Richard (later Lord) Llewellyn Davies, Professors Petersen and Blackett, Richard Marsh and Richard Crossman all spoke. Hugh Gaitskell sent a warm letter of support. Against these stars the Conservatives could only muster run-of-the-mill supporters. Distinguished though some of them were, they were in the role of 'party hacks' and they knew it. Rab Butler and Sir Lionel Heald made the best of a bad job, but the result was never in doubt.

Polling day was on 4 May and the result was declared to a huge crowd of some 2,000 people who completely blocked the road outside St George School. Wedgwood Benn polled 23,275 votes, his Conservative opponent, Malcom St Clair, an old Etonian farmer from Tetbury on the Cotswolds, 10,231. There had been a 56 per cent poll, a good turn out on a wet day and with many regarding the result as a foregone conclusion and so not bothering to vote. The recording of the declaration to the crowd is still in existence. If listened to carefully, a loud mocking laugh can be heard above the general hubbub when the Conservative vote was read out. The laugh is mine – recorded for posterity!

This, of course, was not the end of the affair. On 8 May Wedgwood Benn tried to take his seat in the Commons but was prevented by the Principal Doorkeeper and the Serjeant at Arms. Shortly after there was a debate initiated by Hugh Gaitskell, who moved that 'Mr Benn be admitted and heard since the rights of Bristol's electors should take precedence over the Committee of Privileges' decision.' The vote was defeated 177 to 250 – a majority of 73. A month later Malcom St Clair petitioned the Election Court that he had been duly elected and ought to be returned as MP for the constituency. Judgement was passed on 31 July in St Clair's favour and on the same day he took the oath and the seat in the Commons as Member for the Bristol South-East constituency. He undertook to vacate the seat if the law was changed to allow Wedgwood Benn to stand for election validly.

St Clair's welcome was described in the *Western Daily Press* as 'the coldest shoulder any new MP has had for years at Westminster'. It reported that the Socialists staged a walk-out when he arrived. St Clair continued for two very uncomfortable years. Many in the Bristol South-East constituency strongly resented his presence and told him so in no uncertain terms. But it should be said that St Clair was a young man doing a thankless task for his party. He behaved honourably throughout, fully honouring the undertaking he had given to leave the Commons when the law was changed. He was not rewarded for his efforts by the Conservatives with a better constituency afterwards. Some thought this rather shabby, considering all the flak and punishment he had taken on their behalf.

In December 1962, a Joint Select Committee of both Houses on Lords reform reported in favour of reluctant peers disclaiming their titles and the Life Peerages Act 1963 was given the Royal Assent on 31 July. Wedgwood Benn was the first to use the Act. St Clair was as good as his word and duly left the Commons. The ensuing by-election took place on 20 August. It was a straightforward affair. The Conservatives did not field a candidate, the only opposition to Wedgwood Benn coming from Edward Martell (National Fellowship – Conservative), Mrs M.P. Lloyd (Independent) and G. Pearl (Anti-Socialist). Benn scored a crushing majority of 15,479.

This constitutional struggle was a remarkable effort by Wedgwood Benn. The problem had long been thought about and planned for, with the full support of his father. Wedgwood Benn had taken on the full might of the British Establishment and won through. It is not too idle a speculation to think it may well have had an effect on his thinking. After all, if he could take on the Establishment and win in this way – what were the limits if one really put one's mind to change?

Why, for example, now that the burden of peerage had been removed from his shoulders, could he not become Leader of the Labour Party? Possibly at this time were sown the seeds of the frenetic energy and purpose with which he was later to set about seeking to change the Labour Party's constitution. I think of, in particular, the vital areas affecting the election of the Party Leader, mandatory reselection of Labour MPs and the preparation of the election manifesto. Moreover, the way in which he rallied support from so many quarters may have led him to think that it would be just as easy to gain support in other fields for ideas and policies if they were put across with sufficient vigour and persistence. This idea of rallying support across a wide spectrum was probably reinforced by the creation of the New Bristol Group.

This New Bristol Group sprang from the 1961 by-election and was formed of professional people such as architects and university lecturers. They met together to produce papers on current issues facing the community such as comprehensive education, race relations, and planning. Undoubtedly a good idea as a discussion forum, the Group none the less caused much resentment among some of the old guard in the city council Labour hierarchy. I encountered this resentment as the chairman of the Borough Labour Party. When it was suggested at executive meetings that it should be banned to Labour Party members, I defended the Group stoutly and the opposition waned. While the attitude of the opposing councillors may seem rather reactionary and unimaginative, it does illustrate the vigilance at that time against the infiltration of the Party by elements who wanted to use it for their own purposes. This vigilance has gone today and the disastrous consequences are illustrated in many ways – some dealt with later in this book.

Benn delivered to the New Bristol Group the speech he had prepared for delivery at the Bar of the House of Commons. From the outset he pressed me to join the Group. I pointed out to him that some colleagues were hostile to the Group and I was in a better position as chairman of the Borough Labour Party to deflect this criticism if I was not personally identified with it. He seemed unable to appreciate this point and repeatedly pressed me to join. This was my first real experience of a certain inflexibility in his thinking and at the time I was rather non-plussed. The Group continued for several years but never became firmly embedded in the structure of the Bristol Labour Party's thinking and policy formation processes.

The Labour councillors in Bristol were predominantly people who had experienced prewar deprivations and the rigours of the wartime Blitz. Their main concern was to have people well fed, well housed and their children well educated. To some extent

Wedgwood Benn's New Bristol Group was ahead of its time, useful though some of its papers were. But the grafting together of two very different strands like the established Labour councillors and keen young professionals – some of whom did not even possess a Party card – required tact and diplomacy. They are attributes which I think Benn lacked, for reasons I explained earlier.

Back in the Commons Benn spoke on a wide variety of issues. One of them was on the Single Transferable Vote, a form of proportional representation, in which he said that it was the only system by which the people in the country could have a say in whom they elect and in the conduct of affairs. He also observed that 'We do not print party labels on the ballot papers which is preserving the myth that the parties do not exist.' This is now done, as will be appreciated. A short description of party allegiance is now printed underneath each candidate's name on the ballot paper.

In a curious way Wedgwood Benn was later to turn this argument round. When numbers of Labour MPs were leaving the Labour Party and going to the SDP he, among others, suggested that they should resign their seats and fight by-elections under their new party colours. The reasoning was that people had not voted for them as individuals but had voted for the political party printed under their name. In fact, this was contrary to the reason why this was introduced. Essentially the printing of the party allegiance was for the voters' guidance. It was never intended to supersede the support for the individual candidate.

Benn also spoke on matters such as the problems of fuel tax and road congestion and made a further substantial speech on foreign policy. These were his last efforts as a backbencher for some years. The Commons rose for the summer recess and in October 1964, the Prime Minister Sir Alec Douglas-Home ended his teasing of the electorate and called a general election.

6

MINISTERIAL OFFICE 1964-70

When I was speaking to a group of Young Socialists shortly after the 1959 General Election defeat, Peter Allison, the South-West Labour Party's assistant regional organiser, asked me what I thought of the prospects for Labour. It was a glorious summer's day and we were sitting in the open on Westbury Downs. Maybe this coloured my answer, for I replied that I had never felt more confident of an eventual Labour victory. Those were the days when the phrase 'private affluence, public squalor' was very much part of the public debate. The disparities in society between wealth and poverty were so apparent that I thought the chance of winning the next general election was good.

Another potent factor inescapably working in Labour's favour was the feeling that 'It's time for a change', as the phrase had it. This helped Labour because by 1964 the Conservatives had been in power for thirteen years. One of Labour's slogans was 'Thirteen Wasted Years'. The 'time for a change' factor, however, only works if people think there is a reasonable alternative to which to turn. Brought up on the idea of a parliamentary democracy, where parties rule in turn, the electorate knows it is not healthy if one party continues in power for too long. On its record up to this time, Labour was an acceptable alternative and people had no qualms about turning out the Conservatives after a long spell in office.

Labour today, it has to be said, can no longer rely upon the 'time for a change' syndrome. By the continual infighting, squabbling and denunciations of the Labour leadership and Labour MPs, many electors, who would otherwise automatically be prepared to give Labour a chance, have been alienated. They have been sickened by the internal party constitutional wrangling that has taken place in the 1970s and 1980s. This has been made worse by public doubts about Labour's defence policy and social and economic policies which at times did not wholly add up as being financially credible.

These latter factors came more to the fore after 1979. Now, in 1989, we have the absurd position where the Opposition is fractioned to such an extent that the Conservative Government can put through highly contentious legislation without any effective challenge. Much of the attention of the press and broadcasters, moreover, is focused on a splintered opposition where the parties seem to be more interested in contests for the leaderships of their parties than in fighting the Conservative legislation. For this situation, Wedgwood Benn carries some responsibility, not only for his part in the constitutional wranglings but also because of his various challenges for leadership positions.

In 1964, however, the 'time for a change' factor helped Labour. Harold Wilson found himself Prime Minister with a small majority of four. Hardly a comfortable parliamentary position. Wedgwood Benn was appointed Postmaster General in the new Government. One of his first acts was to establish new criteria for the issue of commemorative stamps, not at first sight a contentious issue. It was, admittedly, a break with past policy which had limited the issuing of such stamps for occasions such as the Coronation or King George V's Silver Jubilee. The new commemorative stamps issued under Wedgwood Benn's policy have, however, by and large, maintained a high standard. But what is more to the point is that this progressive stamp issuing policy conceals a personal battle which Benn conducted during this time regarding the presence of the Queen's head on these stamps.

Benn's concern over the removal of the Queen's head only occasionally surfaced in the House of Commons, but occurs frequently in his diary *Out of the Wilderness*. I find this hard to

56

understand. It cannot be that Benn thought there was any popular demand for this move. The opinions of a few stamp designers who may have been in favour can hardly be given the same weight as the mass of the population who welcome the continued existence of the monarchy and what goes with it. I must say many of my colleagues are unrealistic on this issue. There was an illustration of this at the wedding of Prince Charles and Princess Diana. After attending the ceremony as a member of the Shadow Cabinet I was standing on the steps of St Paul's and looking at the huge crowd that was milling around. Every vantage point was packed with people wishing to celebrate the occasion. I turned to one of my colleagues and asked him how he thought the crowds would react to his views on the abolition of the monarchy. 'Ah,' he replied, 'but they haven't heard the arguments.'

It was a reply which did not square with the facts. It was very noticeable during the Queen's Silver Jubilee celebrations that the amount of decorations was most concentrated in working class areas. This was certainly so in my own Bristol South constituency. The middle class areas had their share of flags and bunting, but the streets that were festooned from end to end, from side to side, and which arranged street parties, were in the traditional working class heartlands. This again is a sign of a certain lack of reality in Benn's experience that has been mentioned previously. National postage stamps are not something merely to be regarded as entries in fine art competitions; they are put to daily use by the vast majority of the population. One cannot help feeling that this concern over the Queen's head on stamps was part and parcel of his growing dislike of the Establishment which he had taken on and vanquished over his peerage.

When Benn took over the Postmaster General's job he found there was a large financial deficit showing in the books. This deficit was the subject of a number of charges and counter-charges that it had been hushed up before the general election and not shown in the accounts. It became a serious matter because it meant the incoming government had to make an early decision about increasing charges to the general public. It came to a head in a censure debate mounted against Benn by the

Conservatives in March 1965. Benn acquitted himself well. He fully justified the price increases which he had to impose, establishing convincingly that the Conservatives would have done the same if they had won the general election.

During these months Benn was repeatedly pressed, particularly by his own Labour colleagues, to give people who were not well off concessions to lighten the burdens imposed by the increased charges. An increase in television licences, for example, was described as a terrible blow to pensioners and others. Benn replied that the possibility of special relief was very much in his mind but 'it simply is not practicable to do it . . . for the simple reason that many pensioners live with their children.' Answering another Labour colleague, he said it was impossible to assist people with their licences if they were on National Assistance because of an anomaly that would be created. There is a reason for resurrecting these seemingly obvious replies from the pages of Hansard which will be given shortly, but first let me give one other example. On this occasion, Wedgwood Benn expressed his sympathy to the suggestion that there could be some concessions on the TV licence for people who were deaf, but 'I have been forced to conclude that it would be impracticable to do so without creating serious anomalies.'

These examples are not given in an attempt to depict the Postmaster General as some latter-day Scrooge. Rather they are included to show the replies of a responsible minister to frequent demands made in the Commons for concessions to different groups which are often impractical to implement in reality. What is one to make, therefore, of his attitude years later. By way of illustration, in January 1987 we find him sponsoring a Private Member's Bill seeking to 'Ensure the supply of gas and electricity for pensioner households; to abolish standing charges for pensioner consumers for gas and electricity and water; and to abolish telephone rental charges for pensioners.' These Bills, as we have seen, are often introduced by backbenchers as political and propaganda exercises. Nevertheless, they are taken seriously by pensioners' groups and disabled organisations. With his ministerial experience Benn must have realised the impracticability of what he was asking for. To raise expectations like this which cannot be realised among the elderly and the disadvantaged is irresponsible and unkind to say the least.

Harold Wilson battled through with his wafer-thin majority until 1966 when he called a general election in March and the Labour Government was returned with a massive majority just short of 100. In the new Administration, Benn soon replaced Frank Cousins as Minister of Technology, a post he was to hold until the 1970 General Election. Frank Cousins, who had been General Secretary of the Transport and General Workers' Union until Harold Wilson had brought him into Government in the previous Administration, had resigned over the question of pay policy, which he thought 'fundamentally wrong'. Wedgwood Benn moved into the relatively new tower block, Millbank Towers, on the Embankment where the Ministry was housed. It must have been a piquant moment for him, for he had been born in a house which once existed on the site.

It was to him that fell the task of delivering the promise of Harold Wilson's famous speech made at the 1963 Labour conference: 'We are re-defining and we are re-stating our socialism in terms of the scientific revolution . . . the Britain that is going to be forged in the white heat of this revolution will be no place for restrictive practices or out-dated methods on either side of industry.'

In tackling the work of the Ministry of Technology, Benn soon found himself faced with strongly contrasting problems. On the one hand, he had to push on with the advanced technologies and research, and on the other, he had to grapple with the problems of industries which were in decline. These were the labour intensive industries of steel, heavy engineering, ship-building, machine tools and textiles. They were industries that were the inheritance of the first Industrial Revolution. Those that comprised the 'second industrial revolution' which Benn was empowered to help usher in were the new technological industries incorporating modern scientific advances, computers, new generation aircraft and a whole range of machinery designed to be capital intensive and thus tending all the time to reduce the work force.

The problem was made much worse because the new industries were rarely tied to any particular area by the needs of power supplies, raw material sources or other factors. By and large they could set up where they pleased. It meant that strong financial inducements were necessary to draw them to the regions where the old 'smoke stack' industries were in decline and unemployment a growing threat. Given a choice, entrepreneurs much preferred to set up in the south of England rather than the despoiled coalfield areas where early industrial development had wreaked havoc with the environment and the landscape.

Thus Benn found himself coping with the problems of a clapped out shipbuilding industry while at the same time pushing ever further forward the frontiers of advanced scientific thinking in the nuclear power industry. His physical and mental vigour stood him in good stead in riding these two horses. Within days of becoming Minister he was answering questions on nuclear power systems and possible assistance in the development of nuclear-powered ships. It was a Conservative backbencher who asked him if he would list the categories of arms and weapons of war which were manufactured by the industries for which he was responsible or for which he had the sponsorship. Benn's reply was an emphatic 'No.'

Over the years while Benn was at the Department questions poured in on nuclear power. The vexed question of reprocessing fissile material was soon on his ministerial agenda. A Conservative backbencher wanted to know the full details of the plutonium transaction between Great Britain and Italy and what was the Government's policy on the processing of fissile material in Great Britain on behalf of foreign agencies. Benn replied that it was 'the Government's policy to promote the peaceful exploitation of nuclear energy by encouraging the Atomic Energy Authority to undertake the reprocessing of irradiated reactor fuel for overseas customers on a commercial basis.' However, 'It would be contrary to commercial practice to disclose the quantities and values involved or other contractual details.'

There were questions on the possible effects on the nuclear industry of a renewed application by Britain to join the EEC, the Culham Laboratory of the Atomic Energy Authority, which Benn described as a 'centre of excellence', the price and source of uranium supplies, the amount of money spent on atomic research, and wage increases for AEA staff, which Benn said accorded with the Government's prices and incomes policy. Some of these questions were from Labour MPs representing mining constituencies, many of whom were sponsored by the National Union of Mineworkers. There may have been some effort by the NUM group of Labour MPs to 'knock' nuclear power because of its competitive position with coal as a fuel, but Benn always fought his corner well.

There was, for example, his spirited speech in a debate on nuclear power in May 1968 when he said, 'we are talking about an industry which we know for a fact will be supplying the power needs of the country for as far ahead as we can see, and which will probably furnish the world's power needs on an ever-increasing scale, too . . . when history comes to be written, the achievement of nuclear power will turn out to be one of the major technological developments of the second half of the 20th century.' Current-day worries about nuclear fall-out, corrosion in nuclear power stations and disposal of radioactive waste, together with possible hazards of exposure to radioactivity by power workers, cropped up even in Benn's time in the Ministry.

The nuclear industry was on the frontiers of modern physics. At the other end of the scale was the shipbuilding industry. Many years ago, the great shipyards of the Clyde, Tyne and Wear had produced the bulk of the world's merchant shipping fleets. No longer. The growing competition from abroad, especially from the Far East, had reduced Britain's output to a dwindling rump. Britain was being heavily undercut because foreign shipyards were more modern and heavily capitalised with new plant and machinery. Moreover, they had working practices which made a mockery of the productivity of British yards, bedevilled for years by demarcation disputes and made much of by a hostile press. There was little sympathy amongst much of the general public for the British shipyard workers. This was the problem that landed in Benn's lap.

The Geddes Committee, which had looked into the industry, recommended what action should be taken by the employers, unions and Government. Benn, in moving his Shipbuilding

Industry Bill, summarised the report's findings in three sentences: 'First, the competitive success of the British ship-building industry depends on the industry itself, the management and the workers in it. Secondly, the Government should help, but all public expenditure should be directed to and conditional upon the reorganisation of the industry. Thirdly, the job is urgent: the industry must not look forward to aid on a continuing basis.'

Wedgwood Benn referred to the many visits he had had to shipyards to talk with management and workers. He was to make many more before he finally left the Ministry! By the time the Bill became law the position of the industry had deteriorated even further. It culminated in the problems of the Upper Clyde Shipbuilders which were to occupy much of his last years in the Ministry. Upper Clyde Shipbuilders (UCS) was created out of a merger of John Brown (Clydebank), Fairfields, Charles Connell, Alexander Stephen and Yarrow and employed 13,000 workers. But even financial aid from the Shipbuilding Industry Board could not help UCS to turn the corner. In December 1969 Benn had to tell the Commons that his actions in the summer 'had not yet restored the confidence of suppliers and customers to the extent necessary to enable the company to carry on its business on a satisfactory long-term basis'. The Shipbuilding Industry Board could not justify helping the company out any more. Benn announced the Government would introduce legislation to provide further loans of up to £7 million.

But the legislation was never completed. The 1970 General Election intervened. Within a year Benn was back on the Clydeside leading workers' demonstrations and marches to try to save the shipyards. 'The power of the workers that was negative has become positive,' he told one meeting. His Shadow Cabinet colleagues, it was reported, admonished him for this pronouncement at their next meeting.

During his time at the Ministry, the development of the supersonic airliner Concorde was proceeding. As the responsible Minister for this advanced project Benn had to endure constant sniping from Concorde critics. They were worried about the colossal sums of public money being spent on research and development, as well as those who were concerned about the impact of the aircraft on the environment. As a Bristol MP Wedgwood Benn had a local constituency interest, which he constantly declared. Much of the aircraft was made at the giant aero works at Filton and Patchway, north of Bristol. Benn stood his ground well and the project survived. It was, of course, a joint project with the French. When the first Concorde was rolled out at Toulouse, Benn was there as a Minister. There had been a little diplomatic row between the British and the French as to whether it should be called 'Concord', as we would have preferred, or 'Concorde'. The French won, or, as Osbert Lancaster saw it in his cartoon in the *Daily Express*: 'The "e" is silent as in *merde*.'

Benn, before the 1970 General Election, also had to deal with the problems of the preparations for Britain changing over to the metric system. This, however, was probably not so painful for him since at this time he was strongly in favour of the Common Market, especially on the grounds of market size for technological products. This may sound surprising now, but he stated his position quite clearly in July 1967 during a debate on Anglo-European cooperation on science and technology. It is worth quoting in view of what his sentiments are today:

'We want a climate favourable to large companies, if we are to stand up to the very strong competition from across the Atlantic. It was this type of argument which shifted the Government's view of Britain's entry and which, frankly, shifted my own view on the European question and on the issue of our joining the EEC. It was the acceptance of the fact that technology imposes an inexorable scale in our economic life, making it necessary for us to think in bigger terms than in the past, that made us change our views. It is not so much that one was attracted by new institutions but we believed that a wider Europe was Britain's proper place and inevitable place.'

These years at the Ministry of Technology must have been an exciting time. Benn was always in the thick of things, trying to balance the job losses in old industries with the new opportunities. It is true that it is said that sometimes his excessive zeal got the better of him. Ill feeling was caused with full-time trade union officers when he liaised with local shop stewards' committees, sometimes unofficially, in a way that cut across the responsibilities of the full-time staff, thereby undermining them.

But his activities did not justify the antagonisms of the Conservatives who began to knock Benn unfairly towards the end of his tenure of office. Sir Keith Joseph, for instance, called him 'the biggest take-over bidder of all time'. Robert Carr referred to him as the 'Whitehall Imperialist'. They are only samples of the campaign that built up against him as the general election approached. It was obvious that Conservative Central Office was beginning to build up its campaign dossier ready for the scares and rumours of election time.

When the general election finally did come Labour was ahead in the opinion polls and Harold Wilson was confident of his timing. But somehow Labour's campaign never got off the ground. It was lethargic, at times almost lifeless, except for the occasion when Benn dropped one of the biggest blunders of his political career. It not only annoyed Prime Minister Harold Wilson but infuriated many rank-and-file supporters. Some even believe it was a major contribution towards Labour's eventual defeat.

Benn, in a speech at Central Hall, Westminster, made an attack on Enoch Powell, who was then Conservative MP for Wolverhampton South-West. It was, to say the least, intemperate, making the deep and sensitive problems of immigration an election issue and something which no responsible politician wanted to do because of its inherent dangers. This is what Benn had to say:

'The smooth smile of Edward Heath is little more than a public relations front for the harsh fanatical policies that Enoch Powell has developed . . . The flag hoisted in Wolverhampton is beginning to look like the one that fluttered over Dachau and Belsen. If we don't speak up now against the filthy and obscene racialist propaganda still being issued under the imprint of Conservative Central

Office, the forces of hatred will mark their first success and mobilise for their next offensive.'

Even read today one can still sense the shudders that ran through politicians and Labour supporters at the extraordinariness of the language. Not only was it an offensive attack upon a politician, whose views one did not have to share but whose patriotism could hardly be challenged, it was inflaming racial tensions. Wilson, not unnaturally, was put on the spot by Heath, who demanded that he should use his influence and authority to prevent Benn's attack from damaging the cause of good race relations in Britain by exciting tension and inflaming race prejudice. Careful not to reveal divisions within the Party, Wilson replied that most people detested Powellism but, 'The words he used must be his own choice. I do not write my colleagues' speeches for them.' That was for public consumption, but privately he gave instructions that in future Benn's speeches had to be vetted.

I deal at some length with this speech because it does illustrate another side of Wedgwood Benn: his sometimes politically naïve sense of judgement on issues. The effect it was to have was best summed up years later by Beryl Urquhart in a letter to the *Guardian*. Beryl was a committee clerk with the Parliamentary Labour Party at the time and was working at Transport House party headquarters during the election campaign to deal with Wilson's correspondence. This is what she wrote:

'My belief is that Tony Benn's speech on racialism was the most significant factor in Labour's defeat at the 1970 General Election . . . In 1970, race had faded into a very insignificant proportion of the total until the fatal speech which transformed a largely dormant issue and a climate of slowly improving race relations into practically the only one addressed by most correspondents. That one speech had succeeded in stimulating all the fears and prejudices to which Mr Powell had been appealing.'

She ended: 'And Tony, our peers in the Labour Party should have learned from 1970 that voters need to know the Party

Leader has loyal support, that there is no hidden manifesto and that ego trips of the sort you embarked upon in 1970 continue to distort Labour's image, cause disaffection amongst the electorate and guarantee the survival of Thatcherism, and damage the very causes you claim to champion.'

How large a contribution this speech was to Labour's defeat will never be accurately assessed. There were other factors. Inflation was a major worry during the time. Ted Heath's phrase 'cutting prices at a stroke' rang a chord with the electorate. (Incidentally, I discovered subsequently that he never actually said that; the phrase was contained in a Conservative Central Office press briefing document.) Be that as it may, it proved effective, and the Conservatives won a surprise victory. During the campaign, Benn strongly defended the Labour Government's record, but was to change his tune in later years.

Benn became Labour's Opposition spokesman for Industry matters, picking up the threads of the major issues he had grappled with as a minister only weeks previously in Government. In the early months a dominant theme was the collapse of Rolls Royce, with the disaster of the carbon fibre blades of the RB 211 engine. Legislation to nationalise the firm was rushed in near record time through both Houses of Parliament. Benn also weighed in his support for Concorde, despite some opposition to this expensive project. Indeed, although Concorde has flown for many years now, without Benn's persistence it would probably never have reached fruition.

Wedgwood Benn also kept a watchful eye on the nuclear industry for which he had previously had responsibility. He praised the skills of the people in the industry, pointing out the enormous market available for nuclear fuel. As time passed, he began to concentrate on safety matters in the industry, and raised the question of US reactors and safety at Windscale. This tended to coincide with the coal mining dispute which eventually brought down the Heath Government. Possibly there was an element of protecting the coal industry here apart from his natural concern for nuclear matters. In the miners' dispute he poured scorn on the Government's arguments. 'If the Prime Minister treats the miners' leaders as if they were not truly representative of the miners he will make the biggest mistake of his life,' he prophesied. At this time he was right. Ted Heath did make the mistake, with drastic consequences for his Government.

7

LEADERSHIP ISSUE

The Parliamentary Labour Party holds elections at the beginning of each parliamentary session. All Labour MPs are entitled to vote in these elections. Not only do they elect members of the Shadow Cabinet, but until 1981 the Leader of the Party inside and, nominally, outside Parliament, as well as Deputy Leader. The situation today is different. An electoral college system, involving not only the MPs but also the trade unions and constituency parties, was introduced in 1981. Its complexities enter the story later, for Wedgwood Benn had a leading role to play in the change, but, in 1970, after the general election defeat, the old tried and once trusted system was in operation.

George Brown, who was Deputy Leader, had lost his seat in that general election and with it his post. His successor was Roy Jenkins, beating off the challenges of Michael Foot and Fred Peart. In November 1971, there was again a three-cornered contest for the job. This time Wedgwood Benn threw his hat in the ring, the first clear manifestation of his party political ambition. He was knocked out in the first ballot, collecting only 46 votes against Jenkins' 140 and Michael Foot's 96.

Wedgwood Benn was one of three Bristol Labour MPs at this time. The others were Arthur Palmer and myself. Neither of us voted for Benn. On a personal note, when I was selected as prospective parliamentary candidate in 1968 Will Wilkins, the sitting Labour MP who was retiring, gave me a briefing on the needs of the constituency. It included the advice, 'you'll have to hold the ring between Arthur Palmer and Tony Benn – they are always at each other's throats.'

The fact that Arthur Palmer and I did not vote for Benn was not an isolated instance. On each regional Labour Party Executive Committee there is one seat reserved for an MP from the region. Wilkins had attended on behalf of the regional MPs for years. On his retirement it was agreed that I should take on this chore as I was the only South-West Labour MP who lived in Bristol where the meetings were held. Sometime later Wedgwood Benn approached me and said he would like to take on the job. I said I would consult with the other South-West Labour MPs. Their verdict was unanimous. I was to carry on doing the job. Benn's offer was declined. Apart from the smallness of his overall vote in the deputy leadership election, I think the fact that he was so lacking in support from his Bristol and regional colleagues made him think very seriously.

He must have realised then that his chances of becoming Leader of the Party were virtually nil as long as the decision rested in the hands of the Labour MPs themselves. But given his undoubted gifts – his superb powers of speaking and holding audiences, his intensely political background – what more natural that he should set his sights on the leadership of the Labour Party? With his attributes, taken together with the generations of Members of Parliament from which he sprang, he could be forgiven for thinking that natural selection had placed him in the ideal position to assume this crucial role.

He was not slow in trying to advance his ambition. In 1971-72 it was his turn to become Chairman of the Party. He used the office to good personal effect, showing distinct sympathies for the ideas emanating from the Left wing of the Party. He supported the release of the 'Pentonville Five' dockworkers who had been imprisoned for contravening the Industrial Relations Act, earning the comment from one of his colleagues, 'His respect for the law is only exceeded by his respect for those who break it.' His siding with Left-wing views became more pronounced though not exactly objective. Thus, on the 'work-in' of workers at Upper Clyde Shipbuilders: 'The workers in the UCS have done more in ten weeks to advance the cause of industrial democracy than all the blueprints we have worked on over the last ten years.'

Benn by this time had become a disciple of direct action, but his final alienation from his Shadow Cabinet colleagues was his campaign for a referendum on the issue of British membership of the European Community. ' . . . The whizzkid from MinTech, busily putting girdles round the earth like Puck in the play, seems to have a talent for sowing mischief and dissension wherever possible,' complained a writer in *Socialist Commentary*. His period as chairman can only be described as partisan. He persistently put forward the idea of a referendum on the Common Market which was hardly likely to endear him to the pro-marketeers. His change of attitude towards the EEC was a dramatic about-turn. There have been many explanations for this, but some in Bristol believe that the real conversion took place when he went to a Bristol Trades Council debate to put the case for the Common Market. The case against was presented by Jessie Stephen – an old campaigner with a lifetime of activity in the Labour, Co-operative and Trade Union movements. It is said that Jessie received such a rousing reception that Benn saw which way the wind was blowing amongst the activists and switched his stance accordingly.

In June 1970, for example, he told his Bristol constituents: 'The world is so small that Britain cannot separate itself from world influence nor prevent its destiny being affected by what happens abroad . . . Of course we can stay out and stand alone, but we will still find that European, American and Russian decisions will set the framework within which we would have to exercise our formal parliamentary sovereignty.' A year later he was singing the same tune: 'I can see really significant long-term opportunities for ordinary people in Britain and in the Six if we could persuade the British public to vote for entry.' Parliament voted in favour of entry that year, in October, though Labour officially abstained. Benn was to start sounding a sour note not long after entry, telling his Bristol constituents in December 1974: 'Britain's continuing membership of the Community would mean the end of Britain as a completely self-governing nation and the end of our democratically elected Parliament as the supreme law-making body in the United Kingdom.' Jessie

Stephen could not have had a better convert. After his year as Chairman of the Party, Benn remained chairman of the Party's home policy committee whose function it was to draw up policies for approval by the full National Executive. On one occasion in April 1975, when Labour was in power, a thinly attended meeting of this committee upgraded a strongly anti-Market research document to the status of a Government White Paper. Jim Callaghan described it as a 'disgraceful piece of research'. Only six out of the twenty members had turned up to the meeting, whereas at a previously well attended meeting it had been agreed to shelve the document by passing it 'for discussion only'!

Only one thing stood in his way to become Leader. Too many Labour MPs did not share the high opinion of him that was held by many in the Labour Party and the trade union movement as a whole. As MPs we were aware this created internal problems. But the essential safeguard of the system was that the MPs entrusted to vote for the various leadership candidates knew their strengths and weaknesses intimately through daily contact in the House of Commons. The only way that Benn could attain his ambition, therefore, was either to change the system of electing the Leader to allow much wider participation by the Labour movement as a whole – or change the nature of the MPs representing Labour in the Commons.

As it happened, there were other groups both inside and outside the Labour Party who had the same objectives, but for different motives. Thus it was that Wedgwood Benn found ready-made vehicles to hand that suited his needs. He threw his lot in with them with a vengeance.

His first move was to tidy up an anomaly in the Party constitution. In the late 1970s he suggested an amendment whereby the Leader of the Parliamentary Party should automatically be treated as the Leader of the Labour Party as a whole. Thus Prime Minister James Callaghan was billed for the first time in this role in 1978. Previously it had been an uncontested assumption. Benn's move was the thin end of a very large wedge, to be driven home by the demand that the whole of the Party, not just Labour MPs, should be involved in electing the Leader. The Party conference agendas became flooded with motions demanding this change. Model resolutions were drawn up and circulated for constituencies to use. 'Off the peg' motions were available for zealots to pull out at local Party meetings when the comrades present were dithering as to what subject they should choose to submit to the annual conference. Articles appeared drawing comparisons with the methods used to elect leaders of other socialist parties throughout the world. All this effort was designed to show that the British Labour Party was the only socialist party that was out of step.

The fact that Labour's method of electing the Leader of the Party had worked perfectly well from Attlee, through Gaitskell to Wilson and Callaghan was ignored. That was not all, for a campaign of vituperation was launched against them to prepare the ground for change. Coupled with this was an attempt to wrest control of the preparation of the general election manifesto from established procedure. This was that under the Party's constitution, the manifesto is decided at a joint meeting of the National Executive and the Cabinet, or Shadow Cabinet when Labour was not in Government. Benn, who had become chairman of the National Executive's home policy committee, was intimately involved in the preparation of Party policy.

The question of the method of electing the Party Leader was discussed at the annual conference in autumn 1980. There was also a report of a Commission of Enquiry into the Party's finance, organisation, membership and political education to be dealt with. I was a member of this Commission, and it was an education in itself. After several meetings there was a weekend 'brainstorm' session to knock the report into shape. It was there that I raised the totally unrepresentative nature of the various sub-committees and policy study groups which had been set up by the home policy committee under Benn's chairmanship. Reams of paper had been churned out by these groups, who were made up of National Executive members, MPs with subject experience, and large numbers of people who had been co-opted. It was the latter who held my fascination – and aggravation.

Co-option, it hardly needs saying, involves not a scrap of election or democratic representation. I decided to prove my point about their unrepresentative nature by producing a map.

It showed the distribution throughout the United Kingdom of the homes of these co-opted members on the home policy groups. Out of a total of 320 co-options, over two-thirds came from the Home Counties, London and the South-East of England. Within this two-thirds, half came from the Greater London area. There were more from Cambridge University than the whole of Scotland, which only had four group members. There were more from Oxford University than the whole of the South Wales coalfield. Moreover, within London itself, where home addresses could be identified, the concentrations were in such areas as Hampstead, Regents Park, Islington, Camden, Lambeth and Westminster. There was precisely one person from the East End of London – living in Watney Street.

When I pointed out how bizarre it was that policy should be made for the Labour heartlands like the North, Scotland and Wales by a bunch of unaccountable academics from the cosy South and South-East, I was not very popular in certain quarters. But people like the late Terry Duffy, of the then styled Amalgamated Union of Engineering Workers, loved it. It was a mess presided over by Benn himself – the arch prophet of democracy and accountability.

The report of this Commission and the various options as to the method of electing the Leader was held at a special conference at Wembley in January 1981 – and is now part of history. It was very bad news for the Party. The impression the general public got from watching the conference on television was deplorable. The scenes of bad temper, wrangling and in-fighting did enormous damage to the Party's standing. As I point out elsewhere, it led to a significant drop in Labour's support in the opinion polls.

After a very muddled debate an electoral college was established. It meant that in future the Leader and Deputy Leader would be elected annually by the Party conference. The trade unions were to have 40 per cent of the allocated votes, the constituency parties 30 per cent and the Parliamentary Party 30 per cent. Benn had got his release at last from having to rely on the good opinion of Labour MPs in his bid for the leadership. That opinion had already been expressed. In December 1980, in the Parliamentary Party election for the twelve places in the Shadow Cabinet Benn received only 88 votes, being beaten for twelfth place by a young MP rapidly making a name for himself – Neil Kinnock. However in January another elected Shadow Minister, Bill Rodgers, turned down a job offered to him and resigned. Benn automatically, as runner-up, took his place in the Shadow Cabinet. He was not particularly welcome, many MPs endorsing the remarks of Leader Michael Foot at a meeting of the Parliamentary Party that Benn was 'spreading myths' about the way in which the Party's business was conducted. But Wedgwood Benn no longer needed the support of his fellow MPs. The way was now clear for his challenge on a much broader front.

But he and the 'hard-left' did not get their way over the preparation of the manifesto. When this was debated at the 1980 conference Benn made a speech that went over the top. It is reproduced in an appendix at the back of this book (see p. 157) because I think it is important for the reader to study it in full in order to understand Benn's thinking and style. Sufficient to say at this stage that it was a distortion of the reality in which the 1979 general election manifesto had been drawn up. During its delivery there were angry protests from many of the Members of Parliament present. They knew the truth of what had occurred and realised only too well that Benn was attempting to bounce the conference into a decision. Jim Callaghan, as Leader, had to seize an early opportunity to publicly repudiate much of the content of the speech.

For myself, the speech crystallised my thinking about Wedgwood Benn and what needed to be done. As it was, I regarded him as posing a grave threat to the continuing well-being and survival of the Labour Party as a viable alternative government for the British people to turn to. And it was only as a viable alternative that we could hope to benefit from the 'time for a change' feeling in the electorate I mentioned earlier. This speech on the supposed preparation of the manifesto was not an isolated example. There was one equally as bad when Benn wound up the economic debate. He declared:

'Comrades, what does this really mean from the point of

view of those whose support we shall seek in an election? They are entitled to know, and I believe that we shall require three major pieces of legislation within the first month of the election of another Labour Government, and I will tell conference what I believe those pieces of legis- lation are. First, an Industry Bill which will give powers to extend public ownership as requested by the GMWU [National Union of General and Municipal Workers, since merged with the Boiler makers to form GMBATU], to control capital movements as requested by the GMWU, to provide for industrial democracy as has been suggested and demanded by the GMWU, and that Industry Bill must be on the Statute Book within a matter of days after the election of a Labour Government.'

It was one of the most irresponsible speeches ever made by a senior politician with intimate knowledge of parliamentary procedure. The only way his proposal could have been imple- mented in parliamentary terms was if his projected Bill had the support of all political parties. Could anyone imagine that a Conservative Opposition would sit back and allow an Industry Bill such as Benn described to get on the Statute Book in a matter of days? For a man who had not only held Cabinet rank but had been an Industry Minister, Benn must have known that what he said was not possible. Most delegates to Party con- ferences do not have a detailed knowledge of parliamentary practices and procedures and this naked attempt to mislead them was unforgivable. Moreover, in making the attempt he was obliquely casting criticism upon his colleagues who had run the Labour Government, a government, needless to say, of which he had been a prominent member.

However, this Industry Bill was only the start. Next in his speech he demanded a second Bill to transfer all the powers back from the Common Market Commission to the House of Commons, also within a matter of days. He then went on to say a third Bill would be needed because neither the first Bill nor the Second would get through the House of Lords. This third Bill would be to 'do what the movement has wanted to do for a hundred years, to get rid of the House of Lords and, if I may

75

say so, we shall have to do it by creating a thousand peers and then abolishing the peerage as well at the time that the Bill goes through . . . '

His parliamentary colleagues who sat listening to this rampant balderdash were stunned by its audacity, some would say mendacity. It was so far from reality that it did not even make plausible fiction. Yet it was the sort of heady stuff some delegates like to hear and use as ammunition to denigrate the established leadership of the Party in the conference tearooms and the bars. His reckless rhetoric was not without its subtleties. There were the repeated references to the GMWU, a major union attuned to his wiles but not falling for them. As a consequence he was appealing to the union delegates over the heads of the leading officers of the union. It should also be borne in mind the importance of conference decisions in the formation of Labour Party policy. In these circumstances, to wind up a debate in such a manner with no chance of reply from anyone else was sheer irresponsibility to say the least.

It was not long before the new electoral college was put to the test. By this time Michael Foot was Leader and he was re-elected unopposed, but Denis Healey as Deputy Leader came under challenge from the late John Silkin, a former Cabinet Minister, and Benn. John Silkin, in fact, was no admirer of Benn and only entered the contest to split the anti-Healey vote. Benn declared his intentions to contest the deputy leadership in the strangest of ways, issuing his announcement at 3.30 am on 2 April 1981. It was the last thing the Party wanted after its two disastrous and divisive conferences. Michael Foot countered by saying that the best interests of the Party would be served if there was no contest. Even a number of left-wingers urged Benn to change his mind, including Alex Kitson, the Party Chairman that year. But Benn was obdurate. He said:

> 'In my judgement it would gravely damage the reputation of the trade union movement if a private agreement were reached among presidents, general secretaries or other senior officials that this new democratic machinery should be set aside by putting public or private pressure on candidates not to stand.'

In other words, to hell with the concern of senior union officers about the state of the Party, he was going to go over their heads and appeal for votes from their members. The election campaign lasted six months, from April until the Party conference where the balloting would take place. It gave Benn plenty of time to mount his offensive. The umbrella group of the Left, the Rank and File Mobilising Committee, which had pushed for the constitutional changes, attempted to put pressure on MPs and the trade union leadership through the activists in the constituency Labour parties and trade unions. It was a campaign that did nothing but harm. Even Harold Wilson, who by this time took a back seat in the affairs of the Party, was driven to make comments in public. He criticised the 'tom-fool issues' and 'barmy ideas' espoused by Benn and called him a 'kind of ageing, perennial youth' who 'immatures with age'.

There was another aspect to Benn's campaign which has now been forgotten but wrankled deeply with most MPs at the time. Throughout the summer months when he was electioneering he was still a member of the Shadow Cabinet, but ignored any suggestion of collective Cabinet responsibility. It offended his colleagues greatly as they carried out their real jobs of mounting an effective opposition against the Government. Benn at this time was very active on Northern Ireland issues, taking a line at variance with Shadow Cabinet policy. He suggested that Robert Sands, the IRA hunger striker, should be freed and allowed to take his seat as an MP. In May he called for British withdrawal from Ulster and even suggested that United Nations troops should be stationed there. This suggestion was not only against Shadow Cabinet policy but even contradicted the policy of the Labour Party conference. During the same month he defied a Shadow Cabinet recommendation to abstain in a defence debate and voted against the Government. That same week he also went beyond Shadow Cabinet policy and vowed that a Labour Government would close all nuclear bases in Britain. The final straw came when he challenged the whole idea of collective responsibility, saying: 'My view is that we are all collectively responsible for implementing the policy agreed by the Party and that limited, collective responsibilities are just a cover for reversing the Party's policy against nuclear weapons or against the Common Market.'

It was nothing of the sort, of course, and after another attack on the leadership Michael Foot was forced to take action. At a meeting of the Shadow Cabinet attended by Benn, he read out a statement inviting Benn to stand openly against him in a fight for the leadership of the Party. Foot's view was that if he failed to accept the challenge he ought to stop the attacks on Shadow Cabinet colleagues, describing some of Benn's arguments as the 'politics of the kindergarten'. Benn refused to take up the gauntlet thrown down by Michael Foot but continued to campaign for the deputy leadership.

Unlike previous elections in the Parliamentary Party the ballot was no longer secret. All the votes cast in the electoral college would be recorded and published. It would, therefore, be possible to see how every Labour MP, trade union and constituency party voted. I had no objection to this. Indeed the previous year, I had suggested votes cast at the Party conference in the elections for membership of Labour's National Executive should be recorded and made public. I strongly suspected that a number of constituency delegates were breaking the mandates (instructions) they had received from their local constituency parties and were voting for left-wing candidates of their own choice. One of those who opposed the proposition then was Wedgwood Benn who poured scorn on the idea. He said it would be administratively impossible. Now, however, it suited his purpose, and was being done!

The advantage for him was that Labour MPs could be put under severe pressure to support him and that the voting of those MPs could be checked afterwards. They could also be called to account, for even at this stage suggestions were being made that MPs who did not fall into line with their constituency party could be removed afterwards by the reselection procedure.

When Wedgwood Benn announced his candidature for the Deputy Leadership very late one night when the House of Commons was sitting, he said that the election would be a 'healing process'. If the ensuing campaign was that I certainly would not have liked to have been a patient receiving that kind of treatment! Normally, on these occasions the Chief Whip tends to hold aloof. His job is to work with all sections and views within the Party. His authority and influence is weakened if he becomes too identified with a particular section of the Party, or too closely associated with any individual. I fully intended to support Denis Healey and was going to maintain the customary Chief Whip's silence during the campaign. Benn, however, changed all that. He issued a statement that the deputy leadership election was about 'honesty, integrity and credibility'. All true, but coming from that quarter, it was too much. The only alternative was to dispense with the tradition of silence, and this I decided to do.

As luck would have it, I was due to attend the annual congress of the GMWU, of which I was a trade union sponsored MP. It is traditional for one of the union's sponsored MPs to make a speech on the work of the GMWU group in Parliament during the year. They can hardly be described as being controversial. Mine, however, was different. The nonsensical utterances of Wedgwood Benn, particularly as he had used a motion submitted by the GMWU to the Party conference as a platform to launch them, were challenged. Nobody was consulted beforehand, not even the officers of the union. The full text is printed as an appendix (see p. 162) so that the reader can read it in conjunction with that of Benn's, but this is the gist of what I said (the reality being shown in italics).

'Let us look at the five GMWU policies said by Tony Benn to have been ruled out of the 1979 manifesto;

1. Immediate restriction of the export of capital – ruled out? *Wrong. The Labour Party Manifesto said, "A Labour Government will retain the power to impose controls on capital movements."* (Page 33.)
2. Reflation of public sector spending – ruled out? *Wrong. The Manifesto said, "Labour will promote an expansion in housing, the health service, education and other social services which have such a crucial part to play in providing jobs as well as in meeting vital social needs."* (Page 11.)
3. Substantial cuts in arms expenditure – ruled out? *Wrong. The Manifesto said, "We shall continue with*

79

> *our plans to reduce the proportion of the nation's resources devoted to defence.''* (Page 37.)
> 4. The immediate introduction of a Wealth Tax – ruled out? *Wrong. The Manifesto said, "In the next Parliament, we shall introduce an annual Wealth Tax . . . "* (Page 14.)
> 5. The imposition of selected import controls – ruled out? *Wrong. The Manifesto said, "We shall not allow our industries to be wiped out by excessive imports before they have had a chance to recover their strength, the Labour Government will ensure that imports enter our market only within acceptable limits. "* (Page 11.)'

I also dealt with the omission of the abolition of the House of Lords from the manifesto, the impossibility of creating 1,000 peers in a week, and the long and tedious legislation that would have precluded the Labour Government from doing very much else. Clearly the proposal was a nonsense. Moreover, it would have had serious political consequences, as I told the conference: 'I ask you, comrades, what would the people of this country have thought if, faced with all the economic, unemployment and social problems of this country, we had ignored these problems and spent the first two years abolishing the Lords.' As for the question of abolition, I pointed out that the manifesto had promised the abolition of the delaying powers of the Lords as an essential first step to total abolition, something never mentioned by our critics.

Wedgwood Benn was ill in hospital at the time I made this speech and some felt I should have taken this into account. I did not agree. He had triggered off the whole Deputy Leadership contest. In any event, he was not sicker than many of the Labour MPs I had to drag into the House of Commons to vote in support of the Labour Government, a government of which he had been a member and was now denigrating.

The speech was well reported and certainly caused a great deal of annoyance among Wedgwood Benn's supporters in Bristol. This annoyance turned to rage when I produced a tape to illustrate the truth about the five policies said to have been ruled out. There was further excitement when a statement about the deputy leadership election was produced by a group in Bristol stating, 'We regret having to say this, but in our view it will be little short of a disaster if Mr Tony Benn, the MP for Bristol South-East, is elected to the deputy leadership of the Labour Party . . . ' Arthur Palmer, my Labour colleague in Bristol Central, told me of its contents. As the campaign has gone on, it said, it was becoming all too plain that many Benn followers were enemies of free speech, disputed the right of MPs and councillors to exercise independent judgement on party and public policy and cared nothing for free representative government in Parliament and the council chamber. Arthur Palmer asked me if I agreed with the statement and would I sign. 'The only thing I am unhappy about,' I replied, 'is the phrase "We regret having to say this".' The statement went out with twenty signatures. Apart from Arthur and myself, there were seven councillors, as well as trade union officials and party workers. I am glad to say the statement got considerable national and local media coverage.

When the election at the Party conference was held John Silkin was eliminated on the first ballot, and in the second, Denis Healey beat Wedgwood Benn by a decimal point. It was a close run thing. In fact, while the votes were being counted I heard of one Labour MP, convinced it was going to go the wrong way, who had issued a statement to reporters that he was going to resign. When the result was finally declared he had to rush around getting it back! Some twenty Labour MPs abstained on the second ballot, including Neil Kinnock, Joan Lestor and Stan Orme. This needed considerable courage in view of the pressure exerted by some constituency parties. They were to become the objects of special wrath from the 'hard-left'.

After the event, a large number of people claimed credit for defeating Benn, and I like to think my speech to the GMWU at Brighton helped to influence some Labour MPs to defy the pressure from their local parties to support Benn. Having supported Denis Healey myself, I was particularly pleased to hear of a nice little cameo in the evening after the result was declared. Denis Healey went off to have a good dinner to celebrate his victory. Making his way back along the seafront afterwards, he spotted Wedgwood Benn in a fish and chip café. Pressing his face against the window he roared: 'Joined the plebs then?' In fact, Benn did seem unusually sensitive about these matters. Returning to London on the train from one Party conference he mislaid his spectacles and wandered up and down the carriage saying, 'Has anybody seen a pair of National Health Service glasses?'

Speaking to the conference after the Deputy Leadership result, Denis Healey made the traditional pleas for unity. But this met with little response from Benn. Benn made clear his intention to continue his struggle in the Party, declaring that the mere election of a Labour Government would not be enough to bring about Socialism. There were some jeers when he said: 'We must not mislead people. We must not tell them that Labour Ministers in office means the Labour movement in power.'

Neither did it mean, for him, that he should accept policies unanimously agreed by the Shadow Cabinet. Shortly after the conference vote, when Parliament had reassembled, Benn spoke in a debate in terms other than those he had twice agreed with his colleagues. He said that North Sea oil and gas assets which the Government sold off would be renationalised by a Labour Government without compensation. This had only recently been rejected by the Shadow Cabinet and the National Executive Committee. Moreover, it also contrasted with his view when he was a Minister. When he was Industry Secretary and involved with the Government's proposals for the Aircraft and Shipbuilding industries, he told the Commons: 'I have always made it clear that fair compensation is the right policy for us to pursue.' Benn's defiance of Shadow Cabinet policy infuriated his colleagues. Michael Foot had to tell him that he would have to ask Labour MPs not to vote for him in the forthcoming Shadow Cabinet elections unless he gave a firm undertaking within two days that he would abide by the normal rules of collective responsibility. Benn did not reply and his silence was interpreted as being a categoric 'No'. Benn stood for the elections, getting the support of only 66 MPs. His days as a Shadow Cabinet spokesman were finished.

After the 1983 General Election defeat Labour's National Executive held a postmortem. I believed, and told them so, that

Labour had received the loyalty vote for the last time. From now on Labour votes would have to be earned. I also said that Michael Foot had never had a proper chance as Party Leader. He was a man of many qualities and capable of inspiring people. The one quality he did not possess was infighting ability. Yet such was the continual squabbling and wrangling that went on during his leadership that his strength was sapped and Labour's appeal weakened. The truth is that the 'hard-left' never gave Michael Foot a chance to lead Labour to victory.

Wedgwood Benn was closely identified in people's minds with this divisiveness. How are we to explain the apparent lack of appreciation that Benn had of how the average elector thought? It could be that brought up in an atmosphere where politics were discussed on many occasions and at a high level of awareness, he thought that this was normal. A clue is given to his thinking in his diaries. He refers to a presentation made to a Bristol Labour councillor and later Alderman, Helen Bloom. Describing the occasion, he mentions the grim building with the leaking roof, the people present as all being over sixty. This leads him to the conclusion that the local Labour Party had become unrepresentative, and how essential it was to make a new Party which could be grafted on to the old Party.

The date of this entry was August 1964, only a year after the triumphant conclusion of his campaign to renounce his peerage and return to the Commons. He had lavished endless tributes on these same people then for their loyalty and steadfastness throughout the campaign. No praise was too high for those who had supported him in his titanic struggle with the entire Establishment. Now they were to be cleared out, or, at best, appended to some new vigorous recruits.

Two years later, after the 1966 General Election result, he comments favourably on the new intake of young Labour MPs, many of them professional people, and contrasts them with the old Left, particularly trade union members. He then speculates that the Labour Party was changing into a truly national party. That may have been the case, until the machinations, for which he was partly responsible, began in the 1970s. At least we have the consoling fact that he was never going to be allowed to lead it.

8

INDUSTRY AND ENERGY

When Ted Heath decided to go to the country over the issue of the Miners' Strike and 'Who Governs Britain?' the ensuing result on 28 February 1974 came as a rude shock to the Conservative Party. They lost. But neither could the outcome have been worse from the point of view of providing firm continuous government. Although Labour was the largest party and Harold Wilson became Prime Minister, the new Government was in a substantial minority of 34 when all the other parties were aligned against it. Certainly the difficulties were such that few commentators would have given much for Labour still being in power five years later. What happened, of course, is that Harold Wilson called another general election in October that year and Labour was returned, this time with an overall majority – of three!

Wedgwood Benn became Secretary of State for Industry, with once more a seat in the Cabinet. Running this Department is not easy at the best of times, and the difficulty was compounded by the parlous parliamentary situation, particularly after the February General Election. One of the themes which Benn began to expound right from the start was the importance of consultation, open decision-making and open government.

The first major debate on industrial policy after the October General Election took place in November. The Government's proposals were outlined by Benn. They included a new Industry Bill to establish the National Enterprise Board (NEB) and legislation to bring aircraft production and shipbuilding into public ownership. The scope of the NEB had been the subject of some pretty fierce internal wrangling when the Party had been in Opposition and was to become a bone of contention between Benn and Harold Wilson when Labour was returned to power. In the end it was to help lead to his removal from the job.

Benn during his tenure as Industry Secretary had enough 'hot potatoes' to handle to start a jacket potato 'takeaway'. After the February election, by way of illustration, he had to deal with the Court Line disaster. This company not only owned shipyards but also Clarksons and Horizon Holidays and had gone broke. Thousands of jobs were put in danger, and hundreds of thousands of people who had booked holidays faced the prospect of losing them. When Court Line went into liquidation on 15 August 1974, about 100,000 people lost their summer holidays, about 50,000 were stranded abroad and 65,000 people lost deposits on their winter holidays. It was a difficult situation, but Benn dealt with it well, earning the unstinting praise of his colleagues and the grudging admiration of the Conservatives.

Back at the Department after the October election Benn, apart from his involvement in the Industry Bill, was frantically busy. In December he had to make a disappointing statement on the foundering HS 146 aircraft, a project which once carried high hopes. There were the difficulties over the contentious workers' co-operatives. And, worse, there was the problem of British Leyland. The company, hit by the increasing import of foreign cars, was in desperate straits. Benn had a major problem on his hands, but of one thing he was sure, as he told the Commons in December: 'I utterly reject the idea that it is the duty of the House, or indeed of any industrial policy, to seek to bring about redundancy to obtain the necessary redeployment.'

Wedgwood Benn's promised Industry Bill was debated in February of the New Year, in which he said its purpose was to halt the long decline in British industry and provide for its re-generation. In March he made a major statement on the Government's proposals to bring the aircraft and shipbuilding industries into public ownership. Throughout this time there was a steady drip of questions about the workers' co-operatives, but underlying it all there was the question of Benn and his attitude towards sharing collective Cabinet responsibility with his colleagues. It was a political bone of contention which some Conservatives notably a new backbencher, Norman Tebbit, savaged at with all the intensity of a half-starved dog.

It had its beginnings in June the previous year when a debate was held to 'take note' of two documents from the EEC Commission. Benn's view was that the debate was to give the House a chance to air its views and that the role of the Minister was simply to present the documents and listen and note what was said. In fact, behind the scenes, Benn was involved in an argument with Bob Mellish, the Government Chief Whip, saying he was not going to vote with the Labour Government if a division (vote) took place. Mellish, for his part, threatened to keep all Labour MPs out of the voting lobby if Benn declined to vote, thus ensuring a Government defeat. Mellish was as good as his word, though in the event the Government won the vote through some unofficial whipping and voting by pro-EEC Labour MPs together with a number of Conservatives. What is more to the point is that Benn, as the Government Minister in charge of the debate, had a clear duty to obey and support his Chief Whip's instructions.

The Conservatives sought to exploit the suspected differences of opinion on how a minister should deal with EEC matters. Norman Tebbit had a number of stabs at baiting Benn, and was joined by, among others, Kenneth Baker. It was part of the cut-and-thrust of inter-party political argument, but leading up to another issue of even greater enormity: the national referendum on whether or not Britain should stay a member of the EEC. Benn had fought for this in the days in Opposition and it was part of Labour's general election pledges. Polling day was on 6 June.

The campaign by those wishing to leave the EEC was mishandled from the start. There were five prominent Labour anti-marketeers in the Cabinet – Barbara Castle, Peter Shore, John Silkin, Michael Foot and Wedgwood Benn himself. They were given dispensation, as were other MP anti-marketeers, to campaign up and down the country for their cause. At the launching of their campaign four of them appeared at a national press conference together. It was a fundamental mistake, since it showed the limited resources available. It would have been far wiser to have split the forces and appear individually in widely spread parts of the country. I say this not as someone who was opposed to their campaign. Quite the opposite. I was a committed anti-marketeer myself. In fact, being the Government's Pairing Whip at the time of the referendum was a nightmare. I was not only responsible for ensuring the Government maintained its majority in votes while MPs were out campaigning, but also had to lean over backwards to avoid accusations of bias about the views of the people I released from having to vote.

Wedgwood Benn was so carried away by the campaign he became euphoric. Within days of the votes being cast he said, 'My bones tell me that we are going to have a massive "No".' This was not an opinion he merely churned out for public consumption. One afternoon in the last week of the campaign, when I was at my home in Bristol, I heard him using a loudspeaker in the road. I went outside and invited him in for a cup of tea. He gave me an assessment of the result, telling me he had never known such a spirit among the people. We were going to have a resounding 'No'. I looked at him and said: 'Come off it, Tony, we are going to lose by two to one.' As it happened I was right, but Benn wouldn't hear of it at the time. He went on his way, having looked at my postal vote which I was filling in. It was the first one he had seen. Benn 'on the stump' could sometimes be quite amusing. I recall during the 1979 General Election, he launched his Bristol South-East campaign from a home-made box fixed to the top of his car. Some likened him to Hannibal seated on an elephant. Others thought it was more like the Emperor Bokassa!

Having campaigned for a 'No' vote and lost, where did Wedgwood Benn stand? It was a question asked of him by his local Bristol evening paper. Could he go on working in a Government committed to Europe after he had campaigned so hard against it. 'As a Minister,' he said, 'I have been working within the EEC framework ever since the Labour Government came in. A minister frequently has to administer laws he may not agree with. I have been working the Tory Industrial Relations Act ever since we came in. But the will of the people quite clearly is that we shall stay in the Common Market, and I have no difficulty in accepting their decision.'

He had no difficulty either not long after to lead the campaign within the Labour Party to take up an anti-EEC stance. Moreover, Benn, together with others of like mind, stoutly resisted all suggestions that if it was right and proper to have a referendum on the question of entering the EEC, then it was only right and proper to have another referendum to allow people to decide whether or not they wanted to leave the Common Market. Such inconsistencies are not missed by ordinary people.

Meanwhile his days at the Department of Industry were drawing to a close. There had been constant internal difficulties over his interpretation of the scope of the Industry Bill.

On one occasion he was reported as telling a private meeting of backbenchers that because of British membership of the EEC ministers were supplicants and not decision makers. 'We are no longer masters of our own fate in industrial and regional policy' he stated, much to the annoyance of ministerial colleagues who favoured continued membership.

On 10 June 1975 Benn was moved to the Department of Energy. Many interpretations have been put on this move, but little account has been taken of the change in the political context of the time. Starting with an overall majority of three, the Labour Government had survived some nine months and few gave it much chance of running its full term. Nor was there much prospect of Labour going to the country again of its own free will. This had been tried the previous October, with disappointing results, as we have seen. Wedgwood Benn had already taken a tremendous hammering in the national press for his part in the EEC referendum campaign. To leave him in the sensitive Department of Industry position would have given a hostage to fortune and run an unnecessary risk. Removing him from the firing line, therefore, was only prudent, although it could be represented as bowing to external pressure. His time at the Department of Industry had been marked by his eagerness to liaise with unofficial groups of trade unionists to the detri-

Back to Bristol with his diaries: Benn in Old Market. (Western Daily Press)

WRITTEN QUESTIONS ASKED TO
MINISTERS & DEPARTMENTS 7.2.1951 – 5.11.1956
(Stratified According to Department Asked)

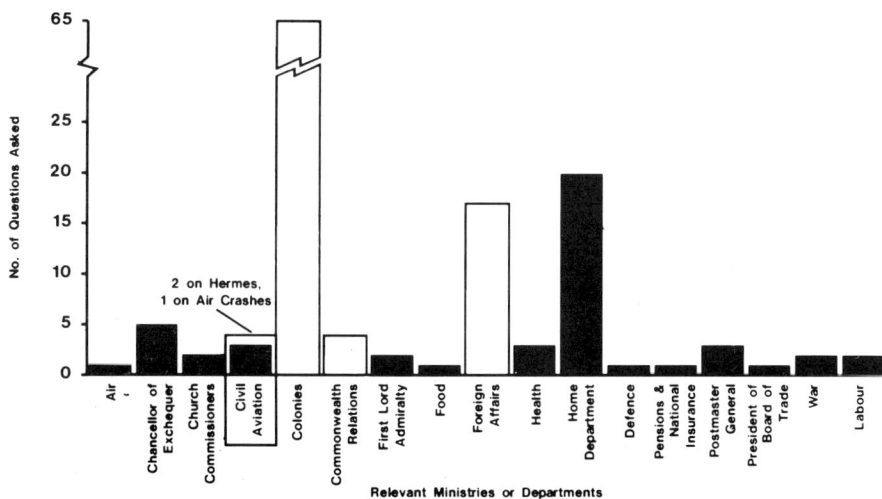

No. of Questions Asked

2 on Hermes,
1 on Air Crashes

Relevant Ministries or Departments

Air · | Chancellor of Exchequer | Church Commissioners | Civil Aviation | Colonies | Commonwealth Relations | First Lord Admiralty | Food | Foreign Affairs | Health | Home Department | Defence | Pensions & National Insurance | Postmaster General | President of Board of Trade | War | Labour

Benn and his wife at a farewell party at Transport House, Bristol, after losing his seat in 1983. (Bristol United Press Library)

ANOTHER fine mess in Bristol South

A cartoon from the Bristol *Evening Post*. (Evening Post)

Benn and Kinnock in Chesterfield during the by-election in 1984. (Press Association Photos)

Lady Stansgate with her son and grandson, both 1987 general election candidates – Chesterfield and Ealing North respectively. (Press Association Photos)

Cocks during his last general election fight in Bristol before being deselected by local activists. (Evening Post)

Benn and Arthur Scargill in conversation at a rally in 1980.
(Bristol United Press Library)

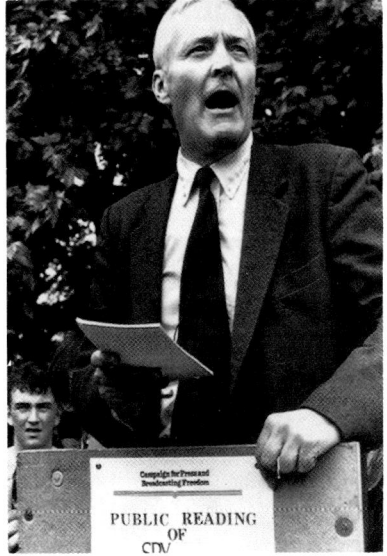

Flycatcher Benn: Benn reading extracts of the banned book *Spycatcher* from the soapbox stand in Hyde Park as part of a demonstration by the Campaign for Press and Broadcasting Freedom in 1987.
(Press Association Photos)

Benn campaigning in Bristol South East.
(Bristol United Press Library)

Benn speaking in 1984 at the rally to celebrate the twentieth anniversary of Militant Tendency.
(Press Association Photos)

ORAL QUESTIONS ASKED TO
MINISTERS & DEPARTMENTS 7.2.1951 – 5.11.1956
(Stratified According to Department Asked)

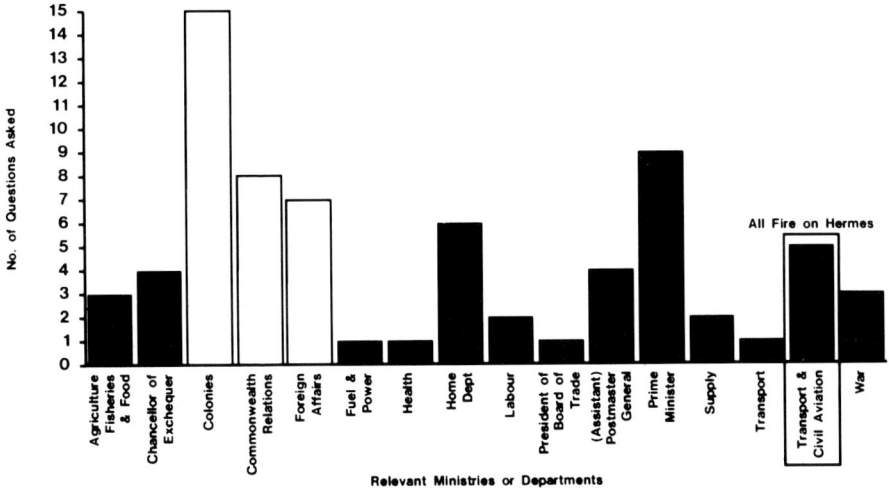

No. of Questions Asked

All Fire on Hermes

Relevant Ministries or Departments

WRITTEN QUESTIONS ASKED TO
MINISTERS & DEPARTMENTS 7.11.1956 – 2.11.1959
(Stratified According to Department Asked)

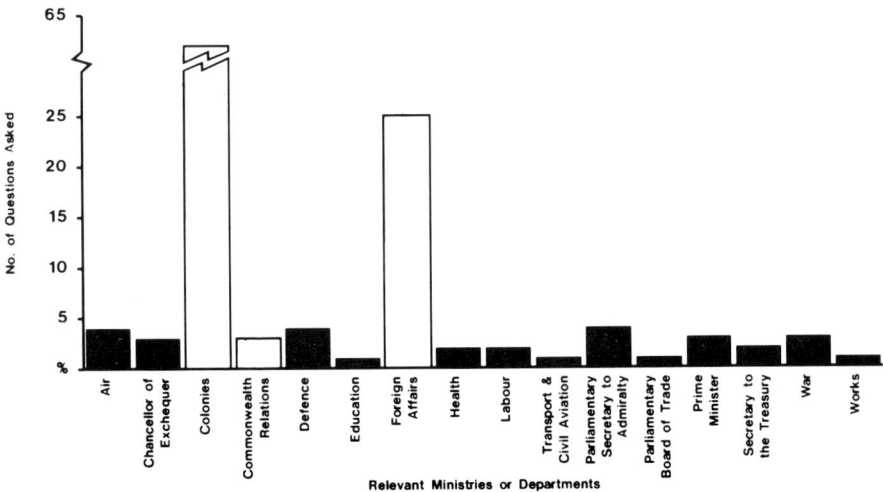

No. of Questions Asked

Relevant Ministries or Departments

ORAL QUESTIONS ASKED TO
MINISTERS & DEPARTMENTS 7.11.1956 – 2.11.1959
(Stratified According to Department Asked)

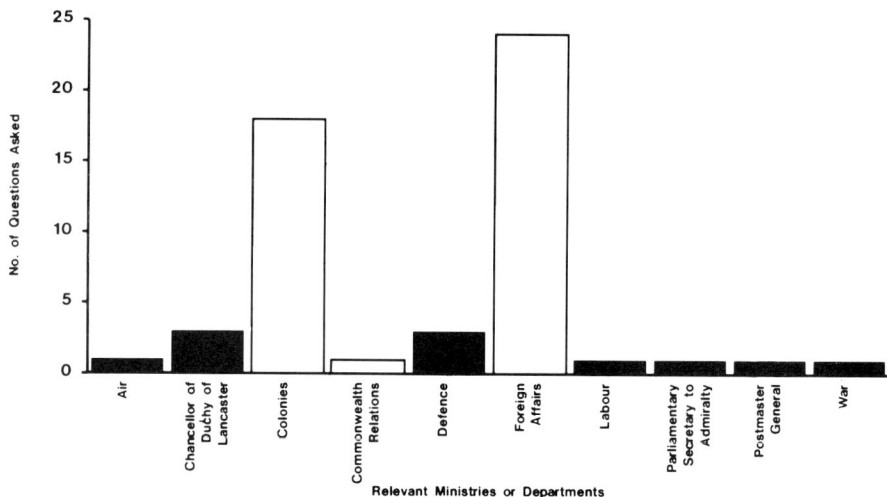

WRITTEN QUESTIONS ASKED
25.11.1959 – 13.7.1964
(Stratified According to Departments)

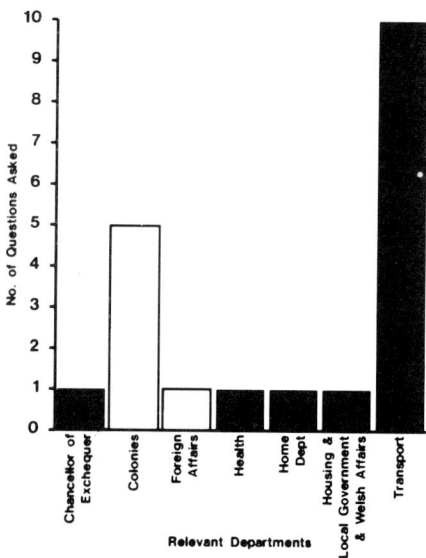

ORAL QUESTIONS ASKED
25.11.1959 – 13.7.1964
(Stratified According to Departments)

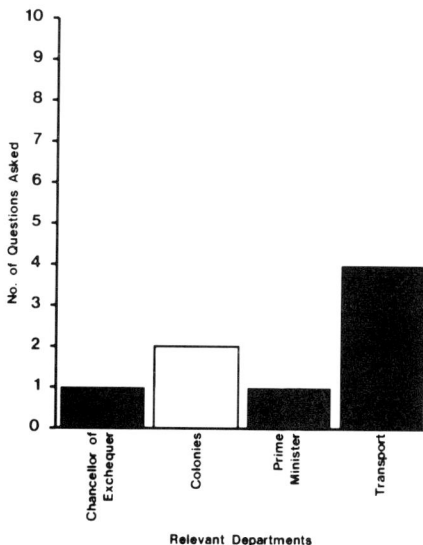

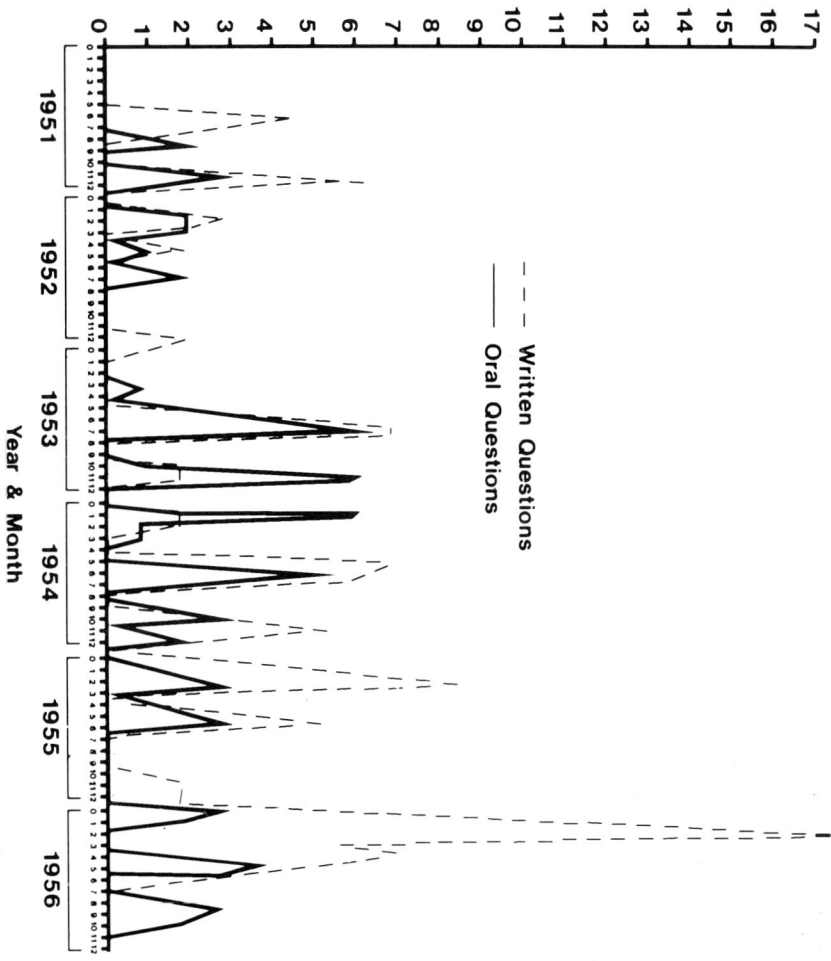

Number of Questions Asked in Any Particular Month

Year & Month

- - - Written Questions
——— Oral Questions

MAP SHOWING WHERE PEOPLE
OF THE HOME POLICY STUDY
GROUPS CO-OPTED BY BENN
CAME FROM.

ment of full-time trade union officials. Moreover, his relations with the Confederation of British Industry and some individual employers were not good. Harold Wilson's decision to switch him to another department may well have been to cut this Gordian knot. Benn's replacement by Eric Varley, a long established and recognised Labour moderate, defused this potential source of trouble. In the meantime, Wedgwood Benn's enormous talents could be used in the Department of Energy. The Department was in many ways more suited through its structure and subject matter to his talents.

Three great industrial legs made up the Department of Energy: coal, North Sea oil and gas, and nuclear energy. The coal industry was long established with a firm union structure steeped in the traditions of the Labour movement and redolent of the 'grassroots' beloved by Benn. North Sea exploration and exploitation was a field embracing comparatively few companies employing the latest in modern technology. Nuclear energy was an advanced, concentrated scientific project involving the kind of expertise with which Benn would be familiar through being responsible for the Atomic Energy Authority when he was Minister of Technology. Taking charge of the Department, therefore, would be a much more structured operation than having to deal with the incredible diversity presented by the Department of Industry. Moreover, hopefully, it would present far fewer opportunities of being sidetracked into various crusades and campaigns to the detriment of the general thrust of the work.

And the workload was enormous. In its manifesto Labour had promised to achieve majority state participation in existing oil licences, set up a British National Oil Corporation, take new powers to control the pace of depletion, pipelines, exploration and development, and to nationalise the land needed for oil platform construction sites. This was not all, for behind the Government's planning was the determination to create a coherent energy policy involving coal, gas, nuclear power and electricity, as well as oil.

Wedgwood Benn embarked upon his new role with typical drive. In his first statement in his new position he praised those who had conquered the great problems posed by North Sea oil extraction. He went on to speak of the changed prospects for the British economy and Britain's predominant position in the Common Market. It was a portent of the battles to come with the EEC. Neither did he lose sight of the domestic political cut and thrust, indicting the previous Conservative Government for having 'failed the nation' in their handling of operations of the North Sea.

Benn painted a glowing picture of British self-sufficiency in oil by 1980 which would eliminate the need for a large volume of expensive imports. The assets were important to Britain's future, he said, and the Government would develop them for the benefit of the people. He also sounded an early warning about the vexed problems of oil-rig safety. Benn was accused by Patrick Jenkin, the Opposition spokesman on Energy, of beguiling the House with honeyed soothing words. His comments, in fact, were a further tribute to Benn's oratory and unfailing courtesy.

But in October 1975, a cloud appeared in the sky in the form of a question from Labour backbencher Frank Hooley. Benn was asked if he would 'now implement his policy to terminate the atomic energy contract with Rio Tinto Zinc for uranium from Namibia.' Benn supplied a written answer saying he had nothing to add to another answer given the previous December, that is, before he had become Energy Secretary. On that occasion the question had been whether the Government would take steps to cancel the contract, and the answer from the Foreign Office Minister had been 'No'.

Written questions are a very good way of obtaining information from the Government, and a skilful constituency MP can use them like building blocks to build a case seeking solutions to local problems. Real political interest usually lies in oral questions where, after the Minister has replied, the MP is able to stand up and ask a further question known as 'a supplementary'.

The Namibian uranium issue reappeared as an oral question on 10 November 1975. Andrew Bennett (Labour Stockport South) asked the Secretary of State for Energy if he would make a statement about the Government's present views on the agreement between the United Kingdom Atomic Energy Authority and Rossing Uranium Limited signed in 1968, and subsequently amended.

Mr. Benn: I have nothing to add to the answer given by my hon. Friend the Under Secretary of State for Foreign and Commonwealth Affairs on 9th December 1974 °Vol. 883 c.23§.

Mr. Bennett: Does the Secretary of State now feel that the views he expressed in a letter on Apartheid Lessons in 1973 are no longer relevant?

Mr. Benn: It is true that in 1973 I said that the Labour Government would terminate that contract. That is on record.

During his years as Energy Secretary there was naturally a constant flow of items regarding fuel prices and their impact on the poorly off, particularly pensioners. Gas and electricity prices were obviously of special concern during cold winter weather, especially the whole question of supply disconnection to people who had not paid their bills. In December 1976, he agreed a Code of Practice on Disconnection which provoked a spate of questions asking for special treatment for certain cases. In one reply he commented on a report which had recommended that the power of the electricity and gas industries to disconnect customers should be removed. Benn's view was that this raised 'large issues' and would require legislation, though the Government would keep the matter under review. In his own mind he must have resolved these 'large issues', for in 1987, when back in Opposition, he was one of the sponsors of a Private Member's Bill which sought to ensure the supply of gas and electricity for pensioners, abolish standing charges for pensioner customers for gas, electricity and water, as well as seeking to abolish telephone rental charges for the elderly. What a difference the passage of time and the loss of office can make.

Throughout his time as Energy Secretary, Benn pressed on with his goal of an integrated energy policy. He was assiduous in protecting the coal, North Sea and nuclear strands of his policy. Some of his references to the nuclear industry are particularly reassuring in these days when there is so much public anxiety about this issue. Some of this anxiety is stimulated by particular pressure groups, many of whose members, having achieved a reasonably comfortable standard of living for themselves, do not want anything to disturb it. They wish to exercise some mild protest to ease any twinges of conscience they may feel about their own comfortable state when contrasted with the misery in which hundreds of millions of the world's population live. My former colleague Arthur Palmer had a name for them: the 'brown bread and sandals brigade'.

Benn was also particularly effective at putting into perspective the safety records of the different energy industries. During exchanges in the Commons on reports of radioactive contamination at Windscale (now known as Sellafield), for example, he had this to say:

> ' . . . I must tell the Hon. Gentleman – this should be stressed – that the safety record of the nuclear industry has been outstanding when compared with the number of people who have lost their lives in the pits, off diving rigs or while engaged in other fuel industries. It would be wrong to attribute to the nuclear industry any sloppiness in safety matters.'

Nevertheless, Benn did acknowledge there was a tradition of secrecy in the nuclear industry and that this was easy to understand. The concept, he said, was born in the highest military secrecy and the scientists tended, however unintentionally, to preserve their own special mystique when speaking about it.

It was during this debate that pleasantries were exchanged about the first appearance of Brian Sedgemore, the Labour MP for Luton West, in his new position as Parliamentary Private Secretary (PPS) to Benn. Tom King, the Opposition Energy spokesman, said he would like to get his welcome in quickly as Sedgemore was not likely to be there long, a comment which drew the response from Benn that all previous PPSs had occupied the ministerial bench as he had no doubt Brian Sedgemore would. In fact, Brian never became a minister but fell foul of the Prime Minister over a leaked document at a Select Committee. I was charged by Jim Callaghan to ask Brian to tell me the source of the leak from which the document had been obtained. I knew, of course, before I started that Brian would not tell me but had to obey my instructions. Brian recounts in his book how I asked him into my office in the House of Commons and then proceeded to lock all three doors so that he could not escape. In fact I secured the doors so that we would not be disturbed.

As anticipated, Brian refused to answer my questions. The only course open was to dismiss him from his job as PPS. Jim Callaghan said he supposed he would have to send for Wedgwood Benn and tell him. I told him that this was my job as Chief Whip. 'When will you see him?' he asked. 'As soon as I can get my hands on him,' I replied. Thus it was that I was driven to Benn's Millbank office to tell him that Brian's time as his PPS was over. This was a particularly difficult thing for me as only shortly before the incident I had suggested to the Prime Minister that Brian Sedgemore was a very able backbencher and ought to be considered for a junior ministerial job! For some-time afterwards, Jim Callaghan would make occasional scathing references to 'the Chief Whip's judgement'.

Jim Callaghan had become Prime Minister on Harold Wilson's resignation in March 1976. Callaghan always regarded, as did Wilson, Benn as a thorn in his side. Wilson, in fact, when commenting years later on his decision to remove Wedgwood Benn from the Department of Industry, said it was 'one of the best moves I ever made,' adding that 'a minister must be a minister all the time with no other loyalties. Loyalties to the National Executive or conference or to anything else is irrelevant.' Jim Callaghan was to have this same problem over the question of where Benn's loyalties truly lay. Within a week of Jim Callaghan becoming Prime Minister, Benn, at a joint meeting of the Cabinet and the National Executive, made it clear that he backed the call by the NEC and the TUC for import controls, 'even though', as the *Daily Telegraph* put it 'every other minister who spoke on the issue made it clear that the Government firmly rejected them.' A month later Benn abstained on an NEC vote on the Government's spending cuts on a resolution deploring the Government's White Paper which was carried by 11 votes to 9. The Conservatives were quick to point out these discrepancies in Benn's ministerial loyalties, leading Callaghan to state: 'The doctrine of collective responsibility includes all ministers, who must be willing to defend the Government's policies at all times.' After this rebuke, Wedgwood Benn chose to absent himself at future controversial meetings of the NEC.

But it used to sicken me to see the Prime Minister of Great Britain, struggling against fearful odds, having to go to meetings of the National Executive Committee and endure Benn's sniping month after month. For a long time I had to counsel that to sack Benn would be damaging. My Deputy Chief Whip, Walter Harrison, and I kept the position constantly under review. Eventually, we decided that Benn could be sacked and that such was the mood of the Party that there would be no lasting damage. I reported this to Callaghan, but unfortunately he did not grasp the nettle. Benn stayed at his post.

Towards the end of his time at the Department of Energy, Wedgwood Benn was heavily involved in plans to reorganise the electricity industry. This was during the time of the Labour Government's agreement with the Liberals. Endless rounds of consultation on reorganisation took place, but always the final stumbling block was the failure to agree the package with the Liberals. It was not something which could be shrugged off, because our agreement had to be honoured scrupulously. As Government Chief Whip, I liaised constantly with my Liberal opposite number, Alan Beith. We had a good understanding and friendly working relationship. We both knew that our respective parties had taken a considerable risk in coming to this agreement and it was our duty to protect it and maintain it free from criticism as far as possible. Quite apart from our agreement with the Liberals, keeping the Labour Government in office was a herculean task. Fortunately I had a magnificent team of whips who supported me through thick and thin. Quite outstanding was Walter Harrison, the MP for Wakefield. He was responsible for a great deal of unsung backroom work, and without his constant liaison with the minority parties the Government would not have survived. Like myself, Walter suffered a great deal of aggravation in his constituency, while battling all hours at Westminster.

It was not only in the House of Commons that Wedgwood Benn spoke up for the energy industry. His speech to the

Labour Party conference in 1978 is a fair summary of his stewardship:

> 'But may I first say one word to pay a tribute to those who work in the energy industries . . . for the very high quality of all the skills in our energy industries which are recognised throughout the world. Some industries, like electricity, have got short-term problems because of the arrival of cheap gas, and certain other problems affecting them. Our reorganisation of their industry was held up by the Liberal opposition in the House of Commons, though the Government remains entirely committed to the re-organisation of the electricity supply industry. But those industries are a source of strength to this country . . . '

It was the last speech he was to make to a Labour annual conference as a Minister or as an Opposition frontbench spokesman. Labour lost office in the general election the following year, and Wedgwood Benn declared he was retiring to the backbenches. I had little doubt what was to be in store for us. Wedgwood Benn's thinking by this time was on tramlines, he could not be pulled back from the excesses of his beliefs. The Establishment bugged him. There was one occasion in Government when he and I were both attending the annual service at the Cenotaph in Bristol. After the service, as we were leaving to march back to the Council House with the rest of the procession Benn turned to me and said: 'Doesn't it frighten you to see the full power of the State assembled like this?' I could hardly believe what I was hearing. 'Come off it, Tony,' I replied, 'it's only TA men, the RN and RAF reservists together with some Sea Scouts and others honouring the dead.' It wasn't the last I was to hear about Remembrance Day services. Years later, when I was deposed at the reselection conference in January 1986, the successful candidate, Dawn Primarolo, said she would not attend the Cenotaph service until it included working class people who had died in the class struggle.

9

BACKBENCH BRISTOL SOUTH-EAST: 1979-83

Wedgwood Benn's declared reason for returning to the back-benches was that he wanted freedom to expound his views without the constraints of frontbench responsibility. There is nothing unusual in this desire of a former minister to prefer the backbenches rather than the preferment of being an Opposition speaker. His actual words on wanting to return to the back-benches, as quoted by the *Bristol Evening Post*, were that he was going to the backbenches 'in order to be free to take part in discussions of the new Government's policies'. He would have been free to do this, of course, as a frontbench spokesman within the limitations of Shadow Cabinet policies, assuming he would have been elected by the Parliamentary Party. He did, in fact, enter the Shadow Cabinet in January 1981 but only stayed there a short time, not being re-elected in November of the same year.

Clearly we were in for something more. Indeed, the same article in the Bristol newspaper mentioned speculation among Labour MPs that this was 'the first step in a longer-term strategy to take over the Labour leadership. The left wing know he would stand no chance in a leadership ballot restricted to Labour MPs. They want the rules changed to give local parties a vote.' This was at a period, of course, before the party had adopted the electoral college system.

Wedgwood Benn wasted no time from his position on the backbenches, delivering a speech in May 1979 he said he had been waiting twenty-two years to make. Quoting both from Hugh Gaitskell and Clement Attlee, he made a swingeing indictment of the capitalist system. Human need, he argued, must be met by expanding public provision and harnessing money for this purpose. A wide ranging speech, it probably enabled him to work off some of the frustrations he must have experienced as a Government Minister.

The following month he made a plea for much more openness in government and said that weak ministers wanted secrecy. It came during a Commons debate on the setting up of a new select committee structure. Benn said the new committees should have access to the same information as was available to the minister in the relevant department. They should be able also to curb the patronage the Government exercised over public appointments. He finished by bewailing the loss of powers to the EEC, saying civil servants preferred EEC legislation because it was much less trouble.

His criticisms of the capitalist system were to remain undiminished. A speech he made in July 1980 seems to encapsulate his growing sense of frustration and disenchantment. 'There are two root causes of our present unemployment,' he said. 'One is the massive slump in the capitalist world, with eight million people out of work in Western Europe.' He had no doubts that the cause of the slump was that the world's bankers (the IMF) had forced cuts in production because of the deficits caused by the oil price increases. The IMF bore heavy responsibility for unemployment in Britain. He then went on to talk about the mass of propaganda poured out with the help of Fleet Street and the BBC, whose objectivity he had once praised so highly.

The general political arguments in the Commons, however, were brought to a halt by the Falklands crisis in 1982. It dominated proceedings. The House was recalled for an emergency debate on a Saturday, virtually unprecedented since the war. It was a very dramatic occasion. The benches were packed. Looking at the crowded Conservative benches, it was possible to tell that many of them were having doubts about the Government's defence policy if we were in such difficulties over

97

an invasion in the South Atlantic. For a brief spell it seemed to me that there was a possibility of returning to a bi-partisan policy on defence. However, this did not last long.

Wedgwood Benn spoke a few days after the emergency debate, when the battle fleet was heading for the South Atlantic. He drew parallels with President Carter's experience over the American hostages in Tehran: 'The Prime Minister must have an astonishing view of her power if she thinks she can bring 1,800 hostages out of the Falkland Islands with the British fleet, operating 8,000 miles from home, when Carter had the humiliation of seeing the inauguration of his successor before the Ayatollah Khomeni would release the hostages . . . ' he said. For Benn 'The task force involves enormous risks. I say as a neutral observer that it will cost this country a far greater humiliation than we have already suffered, and if history repeats itself, it will cost the Prime Minister her position. The attempt will fail. What would win world support and help the Falkland Islanders would be a decision not to send the task force. My advice, for what it is worth, is that the task force should be withdrawn.'

Benn, in fact, had got completely out of touch with public opinion, for there is a very strong tradition in this country that once troops are committed, ranks are closed. When the action is over, arguments can go on as to the rights and wrongs of the situation, but once the die is cast there has always been a rallying to the flag. This may be dismissed as jingoism or Rudyard Kiplingism, but it is how the British behave. I found this feeling very strong when I went out testing opinion during this time in my own Bristol South constituency. The call by both Wedgwood Benn and Judith Hart, another Labour left-winger, to stop the task force at the Equator to allow negotiations to continue, began the disastrous slump in Labour's standing in the opinion polls. There are still millions of people in this country who have been in the services in peace and war. They, together with their families, were deeply disturbed by what might be seen as defeatism. It was Judith Hart who once stopped me in the division lobbies and said to me: 'I think the Party is coming round to Tony's and my way of thinking.' I gave her a look and replied: 'Just remember, Judith, you are talking to former P/MX 830065' – my number when I was a Ports-mouth rating in the Royal Navy!

Benn continued to pursue the matter, pressing for negotiations through the United Nations. He drew attention to a *Sunday Times* opinion poll which showed 6 out of 10 not prepared to see one serviceman's life or one Falkland islander's life put at risk. It must be said that Benn's use of opinion polls was somewhat erratic. His use of them tended to be somewhat selective. Within the Labour Party organisation he opposed the suggestion of private polling to determine current public thinking on issues.

The wind was taken out of Benn's sails on 20 May by Conservative Geoffrey Rippon, who intervened during a speech by Benn to ask: 'Does the right hon. Gentleman recall the terms of the draft Labour manifesto of 1980, which was published under the authority of the National Executive – of which I believe the right hon. Member is the chairman, or was at the time? (It) reads ''We reaffirm our commitment that under no circumstances will the inhabitants of the Falkland Islands be handed over to any Argentine regime which violates human and civil rights.'' Does that still represent (his) policy, or does he say it is different if Argentina takes them?'

Although this policy was later to be rejected by conference, Rippon at this time had scored a palpable hit because Benn was chairman of the Home Policy Committee which had the responsibility for the drawing up of the draft manifesto.

During this time disturbances occurred in the St Paul's area of Bristol – they became known as 'The Bristol Riots'. Obviously Benn was concerned as a constituency MP. But possibly they also triggered off several later interventions that he made on such matters as telephone tapping and the use of water cannon. In February 1983, in a debate on a Right of Reply Bill, he expressed his profound belief in the democratic process, emphasising the power that any group has which is able to set the agenda for discussion. That was why, in his view, both the press and the broadcasters should offer facilities for people to be able to answer distortions or misrepresentations.

Benn's chosen freedom to speak on matters without the constraints of frontbench responsibility also gave him the freedom to change his mind on policies, some of which he had introduced himself. On Britain's nuclear power programme, for instance, he had said as Energy Secretary that the United Kingdom should not be dependent on an exclusive commitment to any one system (this was at a time when he had authorised the ordering of two Advanced Gas Cooled Reactors) but that 'We must develop the option of adopting the PWR (Pressurised Water Reactor) system in the early 1980s.'

Now we heard a different view. He expressed concern over the nuclear industry and safety, saying that the PWR reactor was not safe. Moreover, he was concerned about the dependence of nuclear power on public money and the problems of storage of radioactive waste.

The recantation of his previous views culminated in a debate in February 1983 on the Nuclear Material (Offences) Bill:

> ' . . . the Bill touches on only a narrow sector of the hazards that are created by the use of nuclear power. I should like briefly to tell the House why, in the eight years for which I was ministerially responsible for civil nuclear power, I was converted, first from support of it to scepticism and anxiety and then to the feeling that it was undesirable for Britain to use it.'

The conversion, in fact, must have come about in five years, for it was only in 1978 that he was calling for the adoption of a PWR system in the early 1980s.

Two diagrams are included to show the balance of his parliamentary contributions at this time. One for spoken work and the other for written questions. The predominance of the Falklands issue, together with energy, both nuclear and non-nuclear, shows clearly in this. It was during this period that the parliamentary boundaries were redistributed. The matter is dealt with elsewhere, but Benn was selected for the new seat of Bristol East on 8 May 1983. The very next day Mrs Thatcher called a general election, polling day to be on 9 June. The results for Labour were abysmal.

One of the casualties was Wedgwood Benn himself. In the aftermath of Labour's defeat Michael Foot announced his intention to resign as Leader. It meant the new electoral college machinery, for which Benn had fought, would be used to choose Michael's replacement at the Labour Party conference in the autumn. But Benn, ironically, would not be able to stand, for the rules stated that to be eligible for the leadership, candidates must be Labour MPs. There is little doubt, given the close contest in his deputy leadership challenge to Denis Healey, that he would have been a front-runner. But he was scuppered, not only by the electors of Bristol East but by the manoeuvrings that had gone on in Bristol South and East in the preceding months.

ORAL SUBJECTS TALKED ABOUT AS A BACK BENCH BRISTOL MP 1979 – 1983

No. of Times Actively Involved in Speeches (72)

No.	Bristol	Economic Policy	EEC	Employment	Energy (non nuclear)	Falklands	Industry	Iran	Nuclear Power	Others
12						25.1.83				A
11						18.1.83				B
10						14.12.82	10.7.80			C
9					21.7.80	15.6.82				D
8					23.6.80	26.5.82	2.5.80		8.2.83	E
7					10.3.80	20.5.82	28.2.80		1.2.82	F
6			29.4.80		16.1.80	7.5.82	26.2.80		20.1.82	G
5			27.2.80		22.10.79	6.5.82	25.2.80		10.3.80	H
4			- - - -		19.7.79	4.5.82	12.12.79		14.1.80	I
3	11.5.83	28.1.82	21.2.83			29.4.82	6.11.79		18.12.79	J
2	28.4.80	15.1.81	15.5.80	29.10.80		27.4.82	23.7.79	25.4.80	26.11.79	K
1	3.4.80	22.5.79	(29.6.79) Bill Presented	19.7.79		26.4.82	2.7.79	25.4.80	29.10.79	L
0			25.6.79	17.7.79		7.4.82	21.5.79	22.4.80		

Subjects

Legend (Others)

A Select Committees 25.6.79
B Regional Policy 24.7.79
C Anthony Blunt 21.11.79
D Council House Sales 26.11.79
E Political Honours 26.11.79
F Telephone Calls (Interception) 1.4.80
G Queen's Speech Speeches on: Cold War & Defence / Engineering Industry / Rule by fear (Govt. economic policies) / Women's Rights / Blacks' Rights / Democratic Rights / Civil Liberties / EEC / Labour Landslide at next election. 20.11.80
H N. Ireland (Emergency Provisions) 9.12.80
I Anderson, Strathclyde & Charter Consolidated (Report) 22.12.82
J Conduct of Ministers (Point of Order) 22.12.82
K NATO 15.12.82
L Right of Reply in the Media Bill 18.2.83

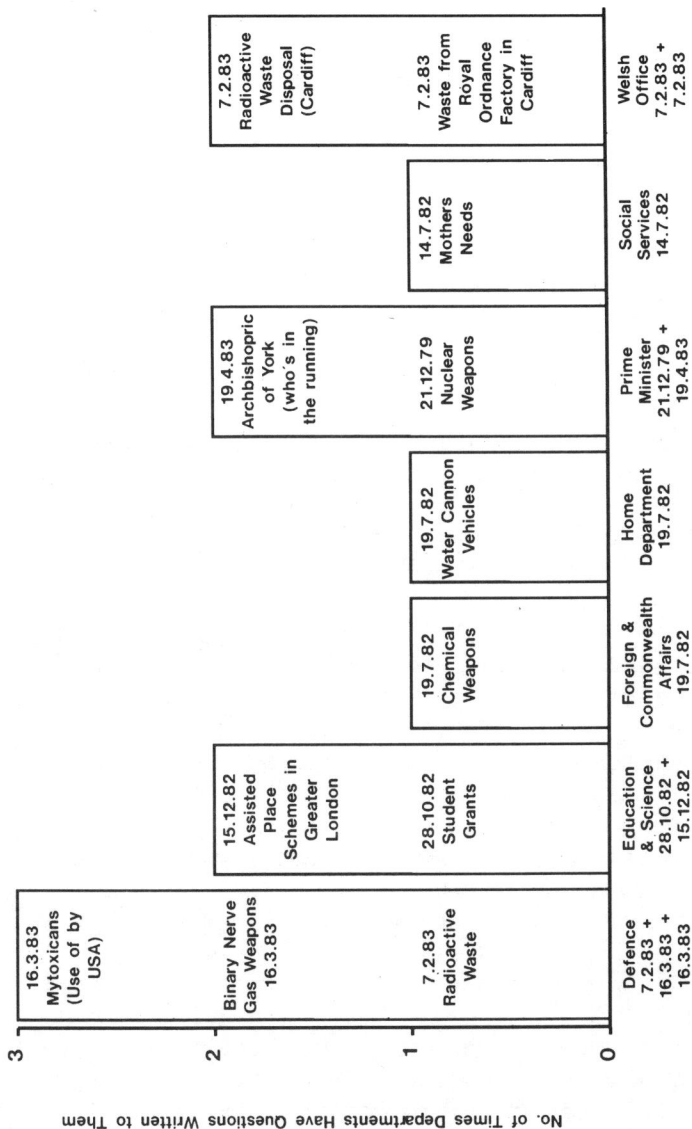

Departments to Whom Questions were Written

	Defence 7.2.83 + 16.3.83 + 16.3.83	Education & Science 28.10.82 + 15.12.82	Foreign & Commonwealth Affairs 19.7.82	Home Department 19.7.82	Prime Minister 21.12.79 + 19.4.83	Social Services 14.7.82	Welsh Office 7.2.83 + 7.2.83
3	16.3.83 Mytoxicans (Use of by USA)						
2	Binary Nerve Gas Weapons 16.3.83	15.12.82 Assisted Place Schemes in Greater London			19.4.83 Archbishopric of York (who's in the running)		7.2.83 Radioactive Waste Disposal (Cardiff)
1	7.2.83 Radioactive Waste	28.10.82 Student Grants	19.7.82 Chemical Weapons	19.7.82 Water Cannon Vehicles	21.12.79 Nuclear Weapons	14.7.82 Mothers Needs	7.2.83 Waste from Royal Ordnance Factory in Cardiff
0							

No. of Times Departments Have Questions Written to Them

10

MANDATORY RESELECTION

It is generally agreed that the 1987 General Election campaign fought by Labour was a highly professional job. Much more expertise was shown than in previous campaigns. Although Labour did not win, there is little doubt that without this campaign the defeat would have been even greater than it was. Labour's temporary resurgence during the general election came as a surprise to the political pundits and the bookmakers. A question, therefore, is begged: What was it that finally caused the Party to fail?

There can be only one realistic answer: it was the scars inflicted by the infighting over the years. There had been a succession of rows over the Party's constitutional changes: the changing of the method of electing the Party Leader, the formation of the electoral college, mandatory reselection, the feud over how the election manifesto was prepared, and the activities of some Labour-controlled councils. The latter's activities in particular caused a drastic breakdown in public confidence – partly because policies were not properly explained or presented.

Furthermore, the inherent patriotism of the British people found it difficult to accept a defence policy which could so easily be misrepresented by Labour's opponents. There were also scares whipped up about the fate of shares held by the general public in industries which had been formerly nationalised and were privatised by the Conservative Government. It should be remembered that the Conservatives knew only too well when they decided on this policy of privatisation that each sale of shares gave the probability of building up a further block vote against Labour. People would worry about possible re-nationalisation by a Labour Government, particularly as Labour had been stupid enough at one time to adopt a policy of 'renationalisation without compensation'. We have seen what problems Benn caused for his Shadow Cabinet colleagues. Although this policy was later modified, a skeleton still remained in the cupboard which could be rattled at will by Tory Central Office.

The head of steam that was generated in the drive to change the Labour Party's constitution gave the impression of a vast upsurge of protest from a large army of active members. In fact, Labour's individual membership has been in decline for years, from over one million in the early 1950s to less than a third of that today. Moreover, if one studies current applications for membership, there is a changing balance in the intake. Far more new members are coming from white collar unions and the unwaged. One would expect more unwaged with high un-employment, but this explanation is too simplistic. The reduced subscription paid by the unwaged is used by the unscrupulous to build up membership more cheaply.

With the help of this stage army, branches and constituency meetings could be packed, the existing officers replaced. Once the key posts of chairman, secretary and treasurer were controlled, putting into effect the stage army's plans was relatively easy.

Of the three constitutional issues, the most potent in terms of bad publicity was mandatory reselection. This is the process where an elected MP, having been chosen by the local con-stituency party to be the parliamentary candidate, is subject to reselection by that constituency party during the lifetime of a Parliament. Other candidates can run against him. If he loses the selection contest, he faces the invidious position of con-tinuing as an MP until Parliament runs its course and a general election is called but without the support of his own consti-tuency party. Mandatory reselection became a running sore. After all, there are as many potential sources of aggravation as

105

there are Labour MPs. The process is long drawn out, and involves maximum local publicity for the Labour Party and the MP.

But it is worse than that. Mandatory reselection, in which Benn not only had his two hands but both feet, tramping up and down the country to secure its implementation, fundamentally undermines our parliamentary democracy in which elected representatives should be allowed to speak their own minds, untroubled by external pressures. It also poses enormous problems for the administration and dispositions of a government.

Let us suppose that Labour had won the 1987 General Election. It would have been with a small majority. The Prime Minister would have had to grapple with the construction of his new Administration. Names and posts would have had to be juggled to produce a blend that would not only clear off any obligations incurred in the past, but also satisfy the Labour Party that all shades of opinion were represented. The new Chancellor of the Exchequer would be receiving economic forecasts and assessments, girding himself against the insatiable demands soon to be pouring in from the big spending departments. Likewise, the new Foreign Secretary would be reading endless briefs and cables from all over the world, apart from bending his mind to immediate trouble spots.

The greatest problems, however, would have been faced by the new Labour Government Chief Whip. Whipping in Government is not an easy task, particularly if it is one based upon a small majority. Not only do Labour MPs have to be present to ensure winning votes consistently, but essential absences of ministers on official duties have to be covered. In addition, the Whips have to service the needs of the Labour Party in the country, where there is a constant clamour for speakers. Earlier I referred to the task I had in servicing speakers for the EEC referendum campaign.

Would we have been able to cope as Whips if Labour's brilliant 1987 election campaign had given the Party power, albeit with a small majority? The new Government Chief Whip can make his assessments in very pleasant surroundings, at his office in No. 12 Downing Street. He sits at Gladstone's desk, with his newspapers spread out on Disraeli's reader and with an armchair to hand from Winston Churchill's wartime bunker if he needs a kip. These historical associations will not be foremost in his mind. His thoughts will be concentrated on how he can maintain a Government with a small majority. He knows that in these circumstances, the Opposition will be ruthless, quite properly, and that his MPs will be exposed to a battle of attrition where every vote is vital.

What will be his greatest nightmare? Not the balance of payments, problems of the National Health Service. His preoccupation, in fact, will be that within eighteen months of the general election his MPs will start to be caught up in the process of mandatory reselection. What effect does this have? It means that Labour MPs can no longer devote all their time, energies and skills to serving their constituents and fulfilling their parliamentary duties. They now have to take care that they do not fall foul of hard-line activists in the local constituency parties. The MPs have to be constantly looking over their shoulders, in a way they never had to in previous Labour Governments. If they do not they may find their careers in Parliament abruptly terminated, their continuing presence at Westminster until the next general election grudgingly accepted by their own constituency party. Even if they cannot be faulted for their local work and their assiduity in Parliament they may still get the sack.

Moreover, if faults cannot be found they may be invented. Hence the emphasis on studying voting records and seeing which way the MP voted. Not only on issues of civil liberties, where traditionally there has been an allowance for conscience, but also some votes are singled out where the party purists say that the MP should have voted against the official line or policy of the leadership. Loyalty to activists' prejudices is more important than loyalty to their own Labour Government.

I was sacked myself by my local party. At the meeting where this happened I asked outright what were the complaints against me. I said there were no serious complaints from the elecorate or my colleagues in Parliament about my work. Just what were their objections? This was never answered. I was just sacked – not by the Bristol South electorate, who had sent me five times in succession to Westminster since 1970. The people who ousted me were, in fact, an unrepresentative group, many of whom had moved into the Labour Party and into Bristol South for their own, not the Party's purposes.

The numbers of people who have done this throughout the country have been much exaggerated. They are a small minority in the Party and trade union movement. But by their willingness to move into wards and constituencies where they can gain most influence, and by their single-minded zealotry, they have substantially changed the nature of Labour's appeal to many of its traditional voters. All this has been done under the cover of an attractive but misleading slogan – 'Greater Party Democracy'. During the 1978 Labour Party conference debate on mandatory reselection I warned of the dangers and consequences. It is as relevant today as it was then:

'Four years ago this month, the Government was elected with a majority of three. I would remind you, comrades, that this is the majority with which the Labour Government went to the country in 1951. It has not been easy. It has put a great strain on Members of Parliament. Joe Ashton (an MP who spoke in the debate) mentioned deaths. I have lost 13 Members by death since 1974, eight in the last year. Only two Conservatives have died in this time. The great majority of my Members who have died have died of cardiovascular disease, which is very much exacerbated by stress and strain. I am very concerned about the effect of automatic reselection, and you must look at this. Labour Members are subjected to far more strain in their job than Tories. The average Labour constituency is very much further away from Westminster. There is a great deal of travel. Most represent urban areas with very great problems. The uncertainty of an MP's life is made very much worse if he does not know what his position is going to be. What is going to happen when local parties put pressure on a Member? I have had members come to me and say: "Mike, I know it's a crucial vote tonight, but I must get away. I face a vote of censure in my party." When I ask what on earth is the trouble and why

they are being censured, some of my Members reply:
"Because I supported the Government last week – because
I voted for the Government." If that sort of pressure is
going to be put on Members, how can I justify bringing
people in on stretchers or in ambulances to be nodded
through, defying their doctors' orders, if other Members
are under pressure to abstain because their local party has
taken umbrage about something which the Government is
doing?'

Although the conference rejected mandatory reselection on
that occasion, the push by the 'hard-left' by the following year
had become unstoppable. Their ground had been well-prepared
over several years. Shoals of resolutions on the subject flooded
the agenda for the Party conference. Labour MPs were
regularly denounced by speaker after speaker. It is interesting
to look at the people who spoke in the successive reselection
debates, not a few of whom were members of the Militant
Tendency: Ray Apps (Brighton Kemptown constituency) in
1977, Pat Wall (Shipley) in 1979, and Derek Hatton (Liverpool)
in 1979 are only the best known. Careful study of the Militant
newspaper over the years discloses that five other delegates who
spoke in the reselection debates had Militant connections.
Clearly there was a feeling by Militant, encouraged, no doubt,
by their success in some areas of the country, that a number of
Militant MPs could be got into Westminster through the
reselection route. In the event, though Militant made much of
the running, others have benefited more from mandatory
reselection. Some from the Greater London Council area were
clever enough to keep a low profile until the system was in place.

Although the parrot cry of party democracy has always been
the battle hymn of the move towards mandatory reselection,
strangely we find that when it is suggested that even greater
democracy can be afforded by allowing every Labour Party
individual member to have a vote in the reselection process –
rather than just a few delegates to constituency general management committees – hands are held up – in horror. Why should
this be? And why should a broader-based democracy involving
each Party member be resisted by some prominent members of

109

Labour's National Executive Committee – including Wedg-wood Benn?

As Opposition Chief Whip between 1979 and 1983, I kept a careful check on the reselection conference where sitting Labour MPs were going through this ordeal. In the first 208 of these reselection meetings, the average number of delegates voting each time was only 37. In other words, on average only 19 votes were sufficient to decide whether or not a sitting MP should continue or be sacked. And this is a dismissal quite regardless of the views of the electorate, or consideration of pension rights, age and other personal factors.

Unfortunately it is easy for a caucus of such zealots to gain control of pitifully small numbers like this, especially when we consider some of the tactics employed by them. Many Labour MPs, when they were able to get to their general management committee meetings to give a Parliamentary Report, have found that previous items on the agenda have been deliberately expanded to take up time. MPs, who have their constituents to see, are busy people. They have left the committee meetings without speaking. Delegates who did not fit into the caucus pattern and thinking have been subjected to abuse. At my own general management committee in Bristol South I heard a delegate, a solicitor, turn round to an elderly lady who had been a Co-operative stalwart all her life, and say 'Shut up you silly old bag!' Ridicule, sneering and mockery are favourite weapons of this new, unrepresentative elite, rootless academics who have been beneficiaries of educational opportunities brought about by the Labour movement – weapons to be used on those who have not enjoyed their educational advantages.

One of the most disgraceful things I witnessed was at a meeting of the Parliamentary Labour Party in the early 1980s. Laurie Pavitt, an old trouper who had been MP for Willesden since 1959, described some of this sort of behaviour in his own constituency management committee. Wedgwood Benn dismissed his remarks, saying: 'We all have difficulties in our constituencies.' I was not alone in my revulsion at this casual treatment of the problems of one of the finest and most dedicated MPs that Labour had at that time.

The average figure of 37 attending reselection conferences

included delegates from the local ward branches, trade unions, the Co-op and affiliated societies. Often there were only a handful of trade union delegates, yet nothing was heard from the activists, including Benn, about the denial of trade union rights. In fact, the zealots never tried to increase the number of trade union delegates, unless they could be relied upon to support their point of view. Sometimes a zealot who had worked himself into a position of authority in a local trade union would then feed into the management committee a series of like-minded delegates from his own trade union.

It is high time that the trade unions nationally woke up to what has been going on, and to realise that the cry of 'trade union disenfranchisement' put about by Benn and others – when the question of giving all party members the vote is discussed – is nothing more than a smoke screen to retain the zealot caucus' control. In fact the present method of reselection works against the trade unions.

The numbers voting to select prospective Labour parliamentary candidates in seats held by other parties were frequently even more pitiful than the average number of 37 in Labour-held seats. These often tiny numbers involved – sometimes down to single figures – show just how much, or rather, little, weight should be attached to the flood of resolutions on constitutional issues that come into the Labour Party for the conference agenda each year.

In the old days, although there was no set ladder of promotion in the Labour movement to gain a seat in Parliament, it was expected that people would be prepared to serve some sort of apprenticeship in difficult and marginal seats before going after the 'plum' seats. This did not always happen, as we saw in Wedgwood Benn's case. As already mentioned earlier I have been told that Benn refused approaches from local parties in Conservative-held seats to be the Labour candidate before he went to Bristol South-East. My own experience was not untypical, having fought a Tory stronghold, followed by a marginal seat twice, before being selected for the safe seat of Bristol South. It calls itself a safe seat, and certainly I never imagined that I would be removed from it by anybody other than the electors themselves!

111

So it comes about that many sitting Labour MPs find themselves challenged, and challenged particularly by a new breed of virtually full-time Labour councillors. These people are attracted to full-time politics by the financial allowances introduced for councillors by the 1972 Local Government Reorganisation Act. They are allowances which have enabled a so-minded councillor to devote much of his time working in a Labour MP's constituency to undermine him or her, with a view, of course, to challenging him or her later at the reselection meeting.

I feel particularly incensed about this because I served on the Standing Committee in the House of Commons charged with the task of considering the Local Government Bill. Together with my colleagues I pressed very hard for these allowances for councillors. I knew from my friends in Bristol how many of the earlier pioneers had walked to council meetings because they could not afford the bus or tram fare. If the Conservative Government is now seeking to change this allowance system, it has to be faced that much of the blame lies with those who have abused the system.

Mandatory reselection of Labour MPs was passed by a Labour Party conference in 1979. Basically, it had been bounced through the conference by two groups. One group was made up of people who wanted to change the nature of the Parliamentary Labour Party; the other group consisted of individuals who were driven by personal ambition and too impatient to serve their apprenticeship.

Apart from the Militant Tendency, those who wanted to change the nature of the Parliamentary Party included a number who could only join the Party after the abolition of the proscribed list in 1973. This was a list of organisations published in the Party's annual report. Many of the organisations were Communist fronts formed during the extreme period of the Cold War. They had seemingly innocent aims using titles including words like 'Peace' and 'Fellowship'. In fact, they were suspected of trying to subvert individuals and organisations.

The reason given for the abolition of the proscribed list was that it was becoming administratively impossible to keep it up to date and accurate, particularly as some of the Trotskyite splinter groups formed and reformed constantly. As someone once said: 'Like elephants, Trotskyists are easy to recognise but difficult to describe.' Wedgwood Benn was an enthusiastic advocate of the abolition of the list, as was the then General Secretary of the Labour Party, Ron Hayward. It was said at the time that protection for the Labour Party remained because individual members had to accept the Party rules and constitution.

It proved to be wishful thinking. Worse, it was a profound mistake. People of extreme views could now join the Party. They were presented with a ready-made organisation and membership which they could try to manipulate for their own ends. To build up such an organisation from scratch would have been quite beyond them with their limited appeal and resources. The lifting of the proscribed list was a godsend. Constitutional changes, removing the election of the leader from the Parliamentary Party, undermining the position of sitting MPs, and getting control of the party manifesto, were their keys to giving the Labour Party a decisive push to the Left. On the other hand, measures to open out decision-making, or matters such as giving the ordinary party membership a say in electing the Party Leader or choosing the MP, had to be resisted at all costs.

The extremists, having been allowed into the Party, went about their campaign with zeal and relish. *London Labour Briefing* was also started, two of the prime movers being Ted Knight and Ken Livingstone. A regular series of articles appeared pushing for constitutional change and slamming into what was regarded as the reactionary right-wing leadership of the Labour Party. Wedgwood Benn was embraced as a hero of this movement. The *Briefing* was not confined to London. There soon followed local editions in major cities such as Leeds, Liverpool, Manchester and Bristol. In the latter *Briefing*, ill-feeling was stirred up against long-established Labour councillors. My former Bristol colleague, Arthur Palmer, had an acrimonious exchange of correspondence with one city councillor after an article appeared which virtually called for the displacement of all existing Labour district councillors.

The pressure on long-serving councillors was very real. I give one example because it involved Wedgwood Benn and demonstrates his attitude when the trouble created by his own

113

beliefs arrived on his own doorstep. In July 1982, Arthur Palmer and I wrote to him over the refusal of his Bristol South-East constituency management committee to forward the names of two councillors for inclusion on the municipal panel of Labour candidates. It meant that the council careers of John McLaren and Ken Legg, the two involved, could be ended at a stroke. They had both given long and faithful service to the movement. John had been a member for twenty-seven years, occupying a number of offices in the local Labour movement as well as being councillor, a point he made when interviewed by the local party and then rejected.

John McLaren's view in a letter to me was that 'If this is not a witch-hunt, what is?' He went on to say: 'Tony Benn is making great play at the moment about the need for a broad based party and a tolerant one in which Militant should be retained – and at the same time his own general management committee, which is Militant dominated, has started this purge of people like myself. It is high time that he realised the tactics being employed by people he is actively encouraging – at the expense of long-standing members of the Party.'

Arthur Palmer and I wrote to Wedgwood Benn saying:

'You have gone on record as being opposed to witch hunting in the Labour Party, and have said you would "fight like a tiger" against any victimisation of party members because of their opinions and allegiances. We therefore invite you to join with us – your fellow Labour MPs for Bristol – in condemning publicly the action of Bristol S.E. constituency general management committee in refusing to send for the local government panel of candidates the names of Councillors Legg, McLaren . . . These public representatives are greatly appreciated by the voters for their untiring work in the government of the City, and to deprive them even of the opportunity of re-selection is in our judgment indefensible.'

Wedgwood Benn replied:

'Bristol South-East has not expelled anyone and has conducted no witch-hunt. You are confusing the expulsion of members of the Party, to which I am opposed, with the quite different matter of approval of candidates for the Council or Parliament. Those of us who are privileged to serve as MPs or as councillors, do not hold these offices as of right. We must be accountable to Labour Party members who choose us and be able to retain their confidence at all stages of the selection procedure.'

Not surprisingly, Arthur and I were shocked that he was not prepared to say a word or lift a finger in defence of the long-serving councillors. We replied that while we agreed that the positions were not held by right, these councillors were being denied the change of even offering themselves for re-election for the wards they had represented for years. We added: 'You talk of accountability. In fact, by keeping silent you are denying councillors the right to be accountable to the people they represent.'

Benn, however, refused to join us in condemning the outrage. The situation was later corrected by an amendment to the Party constitution giving the sitting councillor the automatic right to go on the short list when the ward is choosing a candidate. But the treatment of these councillors was not an isolated case. Moreover, it was a direct result of the drive for mandatory reselection of sitting MPs. It was a drive which continued apace.

We need to ask how this came about. In 1971, there had been a great deal of genuine resentment in the Labour movement over the 70 Labour MPs who had defied a three-line whip and voted for entry into the Common Market. However, this real resentment was fastened on by the groups I have mentioned to put some real steam into the drive for mandatory reselection. In 1973, the Campaign for Labour Party Democracy was set up, and the following year several resolutions on the Labour Party Conference agenda called for mandatory reselection. The National Executive spoke against the idea and it was defeated. In 1977, there was a bumper crop of 86 resolutions on the conference agenda. One would have thought that if the dissatisfaction with MPs was genuine, the bulk of these resolutions would have originated in constituencies with a sitting Labour

MP. But this was not the case. Some 41 came from Conservative-held seats, and there were only four from the Labour heartlands of Scotland and Wales. Of these four, only one came from a Labour-held constituency. At once, one began to suspect that this was synthetic spleen.

In the South-West of England we were asked to believe there was a sudden upsurge of unrest with resolutions coming from the Conservative-held seats of Stroud, Bath, Honiton, Exeter and Plymouth Drake. In the Tory heartlands of South-East England, resolutions were sent by the constituency Labour parties of South Hertfordshire, South-West Hertfordshire, Maldon, Thanet West, Canterbury, Wokingham, Basingstoke, Shoreham, Reigate and Brighton Kemptown. In one's naivety, one would have thought that Labour Party members would have been seeking to encourage a struggling minority Labour Government rather than unsettling MPs who, day after day, night after night, were mounting the barricades in the Commons to keep Labour in office.

The National Executive met this spate of resolutions by saying that the following year it would table an amendment to the constitution in the spirit of these resolutions. In 1978, twenty-three constituency Labour parties put forward resolutions on mandatory reselection, 13 of them from Conservative-held seats. Some of these drew attention to the fact that in the previous year, 1977, 68 identical proposed constitutional amendments on automatic reselection were submitted. It blew the gaff with a vengeance on the circulation of 'model' resolutions on a mass scale. In other words, it was an orchestrated campaign led by the groups of activists. In later years, the organisers of these 'model' resolutions, sensitive to criticism, became more discreet suggesting that slight changes in the wording should be made by individual constituency parties. It was a crude attempt to shroud the highly organised and centrally directed nature of the operation that was in progress.

By 1979, some constituency parties had built up a formidable track record in submitting mandatory reselection resolutions. Paddington, for example, had submitted a resolution for five successive years, Kensington and Tottenham for four years, and Croydon Central, Greenwich, Vauxhall, Haringey, Hornsey,

Feltham and Heston, and Croydon North-East all for three successive years. This was an early manifestation of what became known as the 'London Factor'. That is, the damage being done to the Labour Party nationally by the actions of some London Labour councils. I first drew attention to this 'London Factor' in an article I wrote for *The Sunday Times* after the disastrous loss of the Greenwich by-election in 1987. Interestingly enough, after this article was published, I received a lot of letters from all over the country. Basically, those that agreed with me came from traditional Labour areas. Those that disagreed came from areas which had been smothering the annual conference agenda with resolutions calling for the constitutional changes.

The ostensible reason for reselection was the removal of incompetent Labour Members of Parliament, but that has not been the case. Many good, conscientious constituency MPs, have been its victims. Others have left the Party and joined the Social Democrats because they were fed up to the teeth with the goings on in their local parties. One only has to consider what happened to Labour MPs in Sheffield which was a microcosm of the whole problem. The life expectancy of a Labour MP in that city became as precarious as that of a Second Lieutenant on the Western Front during the First World War. I mention but two of the MPs caught up in the deselection manoeuvres: Fred Mulley, who had been an asset to any Cabinet with his priceless gift, so often lacking, of good sense and nous; and Frank Hooley, a deeply conscientious and assiduous backbencher who took a particular interest in overseas aid and the problems of the Third World. Neither of them deserved the treatment that they received. Neither, for that matter, and further afield, did George Cunningham, the Labour MP for Islington. He described how more and more of his time was having to be spent rounding up extra delegates to his local party to keep the tide of extremism at bay. The new wave of activists that flooded the Labour Party in London did not understand that the MPs they were dealing with were not just time-servers, but men of character for whom there was a limit beyond which they were not prepared to be pushed around. George joined the SDP. Personally, I have always thought George and those like him should have stayed in the Labour Party to carry on the fight, but it is possible to understand the pressures they were under.

There is another aspect of this reselection process that has been overlooked. Of the 17 Labour MPs who were defeated by the procedure, no fewer than twelve were trade union sponsored MPs – a proportion far in excess of their total number in the Parliamentary Labour Party. And this fate was served upon them by activists who shed so many crocodile tears over protecting trade union rights.

Wedgwood Benn insisted on a short list at his reselection for Bristol East in 1981, between 1979 and 1983, saying he was not prepared to stand for selection unless he faced competition. He was challenged by two City councillors but was successfully selected. Even my own taciturn nature was moved to comment to the *Bristol Journal* after my own reselection in Bristol South several weeks later: 'At least this was genuine with real opposition unlike the Bristol South East reselection which I am told was sponsored by Avon Cosmetics.' Interestingly enough, there was an article in the *Bristol Evening Post* in October 1977 - that is before the new mandatory procedure came into force – about Benn's reselection at that time. It quoted him as saying: 'At the moment you can get rid of an MP only by getting him to retire, and if he doesn't want to go you have to accuse him, arraign him, criticise him – all highly unpleasant. I am quite sure the new procedure wouldn't unseat one good MP.'

He agreed then that there should be safeguards. Indeed, he said that ' . . . the local party should not be made to go through the reselection procedure if it doesn't want to.' In other words, there could be only one candidate, making a short list of one. This, in fact, had been proposed by Labour MP Ian Mikardo, who, although identified with the Left, was a wise man who knew what was and what was not possible. He was to pay the penalty for putting forward his practicable compromise. The 'hard-left' worked hard to have him knocked off the National Executive where he had been for years. It was a tragedy for the Party. It is fair to say that if he had remained on the National Executive, the Party would not have got into such a tangle as it subsequently did. In fact, the Mikardo compromise could well have been adopted. The records show that between 1983 and

1987, over 150 Labour MPs were selected on short lists of one.

Benn had no qualms in working with the 'hard-left' to achieve their objectives. But how were they to lay down the criteria upon which an MP was to be judged? In their own lights, an MP should have toed the line on specific policies, but where was the line to be drawn. Their draughtsman came along in the shape of Chris Mullin, a close supporter of Wedgwood Benn, a former editor of *Tribune*, the left-wing weekly, and now Labour MP for Sunderland. In 1981, he produced a booklet entitled 'How to Select or Reselect Your MP'. Published by the Campaign for Labour Party Democracy and the Institute for Workers' Control, it contained a checklist on how to judge an MP's voting record at Westminster. It was a travesty, and for those who would like to study it in greater detail I include it in the appendices (see p. 167). But it should be noted here that readers of the booklet were not informed of the criteria used in selecting the ten crucial votes which were to be used as litmus papers to establish a Labour MP's worthiness or not. Nor were we told what consultations took place and with whom before these crucial issues were decided. Nor, for that matter, is there any clear guidance as to how Labour MPs should have voted on these issues, except for the information given about the obligation for Labour Government Ministers to vote for the Labour Government. Labour MPs, presumably, have no such similar loyalties.

In his diaries Wedgwood Benn shows growing impatience with the old guard of his local Bristol South-East Labour Party, and growing appreciation of the new professional recruits. It is the old-style Labour Party members and their families, of course, who find the whole concept of reselection detestable. But what Benn fails to realise is that if some of the young academics, who now purport to support him, had been around in Bristol South-East in 1960 when his father died they would have knifed him in the back. And having plunged in the dagger, they would have started inflicting the weapon on each other to get themselves selected for the vacancy.

11

BRISTOL SOUTH

The 1979 General Election was held on 3 May. This was the same day at the local district council elections in England and Wales. Because of this coincidence there was a very much higher poll for the local council elections than usual. Since a high poll is said to favour Labour, a number of Labour councillors were elected who might otherwise have lost in normal circumstances.

This could well have happened in the Southville ward of Bristol South constituency. On the same day that I was re-elected to Parliament three Labour councillors were elected for the Southville ward to Bristol District Council. They were Anne Mason, Andrew May and Fred Pidgeon. Both Anne Mason and Fred Pidgeon lived in Bristol South, but at that time Andrew May lived in the Redland ward of Bristol West constituency. When, soon afterwards, my constituency party chairman, County Councillor Vic Jackson told me that Andrew May had moved into Alpha Road, Southville, in Bristol South, we simply looked at each other. There was no need to say a word. We both knew what was to follow. There would be a power struggle, not only for control of the constituency Labour Party but also for the parliamentary candidature for the next general election.

Bristol South was the safest Labour seat in the South-West of England, an attractive 'plum' seat for aspiring politicians. It first became a Labour seat in 1935 and had stayed loyal to Labour ever since. Even in 1979, a bad year for Labour, my majority had been 11,183. At that time the constituency was made up of five wards – each returning three district councillors to the Bristol District Council and one county councillor to the Avon County Council. The Southville ward, with an electorate of some 9,000 was an area of old terraced housing with some tall council blocks of flats. Lying immediately south of the River Avon, which divided Bristol, it was in the early stages of what has become known as 'gentrification'. Long the centre of Bristol's tobacco industry, the young mobile middle class were gradually displacing the old working class population.

By 1980 the Labour Party had finally adopted the process of mandatory reselection of Labour MPs. The Southville ward branch had been weakened by the death of Councillor Roy Willmott, a working class politician of the old school who had stood no nonsense when the Party's interests were at stake. On his death control of the ward soon passed into the hands of newcomers. People moving into the area said they were attracted by the nearness to the centre of the city and the comparative cheapness of the housing. Be that as it may, there did appear to be a remarkable concentration of Labour activists on Bristol South. When difficulties arose in the mid-1980s, I prepared a map to illustrate this concentration. This is what it showed (all three houses being within walking distance of each other):

9 Osborne Road
1. BEN BARKER Chairman Bristol South Constituency Party (CLP). Transfer back into Bristol South from Bristol South-East – 1980.

5 Southville Road
2. MARILYN WOODS Secretary Bristol South CLP. Transfer into Bristol South from Bristol South-East – 1980.

3. BOB WALTON Bristol City councillor for Southville ward since 1983. Vice-chairman Land and Admin. Committee. Transfer Bristol South from Bristol West – 1980.

4. GEORGE MICKLEWRIGHT City councillor for Windmill Hill ward since 1979. Chairman Housing Committee.

Secretary Bristol City Council Labour Group. Transfer into Bristol South from Bristol West – 1983.

5. SUE HODKINSON Avon County councillor for Southville ward since 1981. Secretary Avon County Labour Group. Transfer into Bristol South from Bristol West – 1983.

36 Alpha Road

6. ANDREW MAY Bristol City councillor for Southville ward since 1979. Chairman Planning Committee and Vice-chairman Resources Committee. Deputy Leader of Bristol City Council Labour Group. Transfer into Bristol South from Bristol West – 1982. Labour Party membership was retained in Bristol West for a year after he moved into Bristol South.

7. KEN FYFFE Membership secretary Bristol South CLP. Transfer into Bristol South from Bristol West 1981.

Obviously things have changed since the list was prepared, but this is how they stood at the time. Labour groups, it should be explained, are the private meetings of the Labour councillors where they discuss council business and policy before formal council meetings. There is nothing sinister in this. Other parties, including the Conservatives and Liberals, have similar groups, but the officers wield considerable power and, in terms of local politics, they are very influential positions.

A mandatory reselection process in the Bristol South CLP took place in 1981, culminating in a selection conference held on 13 December 1981. Originally there were four candidates: Andrew May and George Micklewright, who appear in the list, Trevor Morgan, who lived in Bristol and was a building worker, and myself. George Mickelwright withdrew before the day and issued a statement saying that the only ward which had taken the reselection process seriously was Southville – that is the ward in which he and six prominent officers of the Party lived. He asked his supporters to transfer their allegiance to Andrew May as the most suitable candidate to represent the constituency. In other words, the guns against me had not only been primed but had been cocked. In the event they missed the target, i.e. me. There were 49 delegates eligible to attend the selection conference, and though the whole of the Southville delegates supported May, I won easily.

In my speech at the selection conference I stressed my work for the Labour Party in Bristol over the years. When I had been Chairman of the Borough Labour Party from 1961-63, I had visited and worked in every ward in Bristol. That when I had first been elected, it had been understood that I could not attend midweek meetings when the Commons was in session. In case all this may sound to the reader somewhat dull and mundane, it has to be remembered that there were those at the conference who would either not know or would choose to ignore my record for their own purposes. That was why I informed them of my voting record in Parliament. In the six parliamentary sessions from 1974 through to the beginning of 1979, there had been 1,304 possible votes – I voted in all but six, and of these on three occasions I had been officially paired.

I had won through the reselection on that occasion, but things were to deteriorate from then on, particularly because of the effect of the redistribution of parliamentary constituencies. Early in the 1960s, the Parliamentary Boundary Commission, whose function it is to examine the size and geographical boundaries of constituencies, had produced proposals for the Bristol area. I was asked to examine these by the Labour Party Regional Office and advised on what I thought would be the arrangement which gave the best outcome for Labour. There is nothing wrong or dishonourable about this since each political party tries to achieve the best result for itself. In the end, of course, it is for the Boundary Commission to decide, but, as it happened, they eventually adopted the scheme that I had prepared for the Labour Party.

The proposals generated friction between three of the five Labour MPs who represented Bristol at the time. In particular, Wedgwood Benn clashed at a public inquiry with Arthur Palmer (Bristol Central) and Will Wilkins who was then the MP for Bristol South. Benn supported an alternative scheme put forward by his own Bristol South-East constituency party. The outcome was that the new boundaries were established and Benn thought his new Bristol South-East seat had become a super-marginal. I was never able to take this idea seriously, having been so closely involved in the whole matter, but the idea took firm hold among his supporters in Bristol and the rest of the country. As a result, during the February 1974 General Election, Bristol South-East was flooded with workers from different parts of the country, including miners from South Wales. He was returned with a majority of 7,912, and in the second general election in October his majority rose to 9,373. Labour's results had benefited from the fact that the Boundary Commission's changes had concentrated the Tory strength into the already strong Conservative Bristol West.

Some years later, I mentioned to Benn the part that I had played in this redistribution. He went very quiet. I pointed out to him that I had no personal interest in Bristol South at the time. But I got the impression that he thought I had deliberately suggested options that would damage his constituency. The size of his majorities are convincing proof that this was not the case.

But we hadn't finished with the Boundary Review. The Commission appeared in April 1980 with new proposals and caused widespread consternation. Without any doubt, politically, the only certain Labour seat in Bristol under the proposals would be Bristol South, the seat for which I was now the MP. Under the changes some parts of the old Bristol South-East came into Bristol South, and, similarly, some parts of Bristol South went into a newly-defined Bristol East. It meant that Benn and I both had claims on the new Bristol South and East seats. Benn, in fact, also had an option on another seat adjoining his old constituency but this had no direct bearing on what was to happen in Bristol South. When the redistributed seats had to select their candidates we were duly asked, by Labour's South-West Regional Organiser, to state our intentions as to which seats we wished to stand for, although the dates of the selection conferences had not been fixed. It was a matter that needed considerable thought.

It suddenly occurred to me that if Bristol East selected first, and both Benn and I appeared at the selection, all that Benn's supporters had to do was vote for me. I would then be locked in as the Bristol East candidate, giving Benn a completely free run in the safer Bristol South seat as he was the only person apart from myself with a claim. I replied to the Regional Organiser that while I had a technical claim on Bristol East, I considered I had no moral claim: I only wished to be considered for Bristol South. In fact, when the date order for the selection conferences was decided Bristol South was the first.

Benn's complaint had been that in the redistribution of the seats the majority of his electorate had gone to the new Bristol South. The facts do not bear this out. They show that in the new Bristol South over three-quarters of the electorate came from my old seat. In the light of this, it is difficult to understand remarks attributed to Wedgwood Benn in his profile feature in *The House* magazine, the weekly journal of the Houses of Parliament, on 11 June 1986. 'I must be the only person who has fought and won four by-elections and every General Election since 1951: I've fought fourteen and won thirteen, but I don't really count that as a defeat, as it wasn't my seat, but I don't protest for reasons of loyalty.'

The selection conference was held at Hartcliffe Labour Club on Saturday, 7 May 1983. It should come as no particular surprise that a lot of preparatory work had gone on before this. To have gone into battle without surveying the ground and mustering the troops would have been to stretch the limits of faith into the realm of reckless folly. What, therefore, lay before the two contestants? The new Bristol South constituency was now made up of eight wards: two of the wards with a large membership were for Benn – Southville, already described, and Windmill Hill, an inner city ward, mainly of old terraced housing and formerly in Benn's old constituency. Two other wards were delicately balanced and could favour either candidate: Knowle, an area of good Victorian housing and prewar council housing, and Whitchurch Park, which was half council estate and part of a large private estate from Benn's old constituency. The four other wards favoured me, but had smaller memberships. They were: Bedminster, an area of Victorian terrace and middle class housing, Bishopsworth, middle class houses with some prewar council estates, Filwood, predominantly a prewar council estate, and Hartcliffe, basically a huge postwar council estate.

That was the geography, but what about the votes? The delegates to the general management committee from the trade unions, co-operative and socialist societies were estimated to split more or less evenly between Benn and Cocks supporters. It soon became clear that whoever got the support of the two wards which were delicately balanced – Knowle and Whitchurch Park – would be virtually home and dry when the selection meeting vote was taken. A serious loophole in the Labour Party's procedure for selection is that although delegates taking part have to have been Party members of the constituency for twelve months previous to selection, members who select those delegates do not have to fulful this requirement. They can be members for a day, or even less. With this in mind, between November 1982 and February 1983 a number of known Cocks supporters living in the Knowle and Whitchurch Park wards were quietly recruited into the Labour Party. Their applications were processed through the Bristol South CLP a few at a time.

Benn's supporters, either not knowing of the late enrolments or not appreciating their significance, are believed to have sent him a message that all was well and that the seat would be delivered to him. Benn made a declaration of loyalty to the City of Bristol, saying he wanted to stay as a Bristol MP. It was hardly surprising, considering another aspect that occurred during this campaign which had been seized upon by the national press. They reported that Wedgwood Benn was considering safe seats in other parts of the country, hardly a situation which would endear him to people in Bristol. Newport was mentioned, the old seat having been divided into two new seats. Newham was also floated. There were also reports of him showing an interest in the new Scottish seat of Livingstone. The *Daily Mirror* featured the story under the headline 'MacBenn', and showed a photograph of him to which a Scottish bonnet had been added. In another story, Bill Gilby, secretary of the West Lothian constituency Labour Party, and chairman of the organisation committee of the Labour Party in Scotland, is quoted as saying: 'Mr Benn would have every bit as much right as Mr Cook to lay claim to Livingstone, Mr Cook does not have any territorial claim there either'. Robin Cook, who now represents the seat, to which he had a substantial claim, was worried about these soundings and discussed the matter with me on more than one occasion.

Another factor was – the number of delegates to be allowed to go to the general management committee, that is, the selection committee. Clearly where a new constituency is created the matter has to be settled before the new constituency management committee can be established. A joint meeting was held on 20 February 1983 at the Party's regional office, between representatives from Bristol South and the old Bristol South-East constituency, where the appointment of delegates was thrashed out. Bristol South's officers, sympathetic to Cocks, argued their prepared case. If they won it would mean that a ward with 149 members would in fact have only two more delegates than a ward with 26 members. By this means the South-ville and Windmill Hill wards with pro-Benn delegations could be kept down to a manageable size. The proposal was accepted.

When the wards came to select their delegates, Southville and Windmill Hill wards, as expected, appointed pro-Benn people; Bedminster, Bishopsworth, Filwood, and Hartcliffe wards all appointed pro-Cocks delegates. The vital meetings of Knowle and Whitchurch Park chose as follows: Knowle 4-2 in favour of Cocks, and Whitchurch Park was 6-0 in favour of Cocks! It meant that from these two wards 10 would back Cocks and only two would be in favour of Benn. Allegations of vote-rigging and unfair practice flew. The Party regional head-quarters was called in by Benn supporters to investigate their complaints but all was found in order. The delegations stood. We had beaten the Bennite insurgents at their own game.

The day of the selection conference came. There were 107 delegates present. Benn and I drew lots for order of speaking and he went first. We both spoke for fifteen minutes and answered questions for twenty minutes. I was chosen. After-wards delegates talked among themselves. It was reported to me that my opponents said mine would be a 'Pyrrhic victory', that I would have nothing but 'hassle' from now on. It came as no surprise. I hardly needed telling that things from now on would not be easy and that I would not be lightly forgiven for denying Benn the safest Labour seat in the region.

As for Benn himself, he was chosen to fight Bristol East and lost in the ensuing 1983 General Election by 1,789 votes. Thus, as we have seen, he was out of Parliament at a crucial time when the Labour Party was electing a new leader. He was ineligible to stand and had to watch from the sidelines when Neil Kinnock and Roy Hattersley were, respectively, elected Leader and Deputy Leader. Benn's generation had been bypassed. Much will depend in the future as to whether or not Benn can reconcile himself to this fact and join in supporting Neil Kinnock.

12

MILITANT

If one had to select from all the activities of Wedgwood Benn the one that deserves criticism above all others, I think, it would have to be the way in which he persistently tried to block those who wanted to take action against what is known as the Militant Tendency. The difficulty of pinning down this group – and the problem of drawing them from the shadows to be dealt with – was amply demonstrated during the efforts by Labour's National Executive to get to grips with them in the 1980s. They were, and are, a curse. The origins of the Tendency go back to the mid-1950s when a small body called the Revolutionary Socialist League tried to infiltrate into the Labour Party. In 1964 the leaders of the RSL began publishing *Militant*, and it is around this weekly newspaper that they now gather, calling for crackpot policies which no sane politician wants and can never be implemented.

They are nothing but infantile political troublemakers bent upon undermining the democratic process. Although attention has been concentrated on the key figures who were associated with the publication of the *Militant* newspaper and the situation in Liverpool, the extent of Militant's influence was widespread. I document it here because during my period as Labour Chief Whip a considerable amount of information was given to me which I was able to pass on to the Labour leadership and it is time that it was made public.

Militant members were entrenched in Wedgwood Benn's

Bristol's South-East constituency Labour Party. This was clearly seen in the notes sent to me by John McLaren at the time of the row which Arthur Palmer and I had with Benn. It will be recalled that Bristol South-East CLP refused to send forward the names of long-serving councillors for inclusion in the panel of council candidates. In the course of his correspondence to me, John McLaren described what happened during that relevant meeting when he was turned down.

Before McLaren's case came up for debate he said there was a discussion on a resolution that stated the belief that the Labour Party was a broadly based party, drawing its strengths from the views of its membership and from a wide range of groups. The resolution therefore rejected any proposals for expulsions or the registration or de-registration of groups within the Party.

Another resolution was moved which specifically recognised the Militant Tendency as an integral part of the Party.

John McLaren continued:

'I was sitting amongst a group of ten or so Militant supporters who were organised by Bryan Beckingham, the regional organiser of the Militant Tendency. He was organising who was to speak and which particular points they should speak to. Wedgwood Benn spoke strongly in favour of the resolutions (including the one that supported Militant's continued membership of the Party) and the debate was dominated by speakers from Militant. I was the only speaker against the resolutions . . . I stressed my opinion that the first priority we have as a Party is to win people back who had until recently been loyal and long-standing Labour voters. The resolutions were carried with only six voting against (there were about forty delegates present).'

The influence of Militant is clear here, and the Labour Party nationally was made aware of this danger by a number of people. I had an occasion to complain to the Regional Organiser about Bryan Beckingham's behaviour at the annual conference of the Party's South-West region. Sitting on the platform I suddenly noticed that he had risen from his seat at the press table and was orchestrating speakers in the floor of the hall during a debate, just as described by John McLaren. The reply I received from the Regional Organiser was that Beckingham had got a press pass, representing Militant Newspapers!

The registration of groups referred to may need a short explanation. In March 1980, Labour's National Executive circulated a questionnaire to all groups made up of Labour Party members asking for details of the organisation, membership and finance. I analysed the answers from some twenty-one groups that replied, including Militant. All the replies gave details of officers: thirteen of them said they employed nobody full time. Twelve had no premises, thirteen published their accounts. In addition, one group had no income. Apart from Militant, the maximum number of full-time workers reported by a group was Independent Labour Publications with two and a half. No group had more than one set of premises. Militant had a different story to tell. They admitted to having 50 full-time workers, two sets of premises, and they did not publish accounts!

Yet still the Labour Party prevaricated about taking action. Anybody holding the position of Labour Chief Whip in Parliament receives feedback from all over the country about what is going on in Labour circles. So concerned did I become about the activities of Militant that I wrote to the Party's General Secretary in November 1981 about the position of the Labour Party in Liverpool and called for an inquiry which was rejected. If only this opportunity had been taken the whole history of the Party, considering the problems it had with Militant, might have been different. I pointed out the following facts:

1. In the 1979 General Election, Liverpool had returned five Labour MPs.

2. Since then, of these five MPs, three had defected from the Party, including one who had not been reselected. I pointed out that the odds against this happening, without the ruinous intervention of Militant, were 1,830 to 1, a calculation done for me by a local university statistician.

I also mentioned that we had lost the Liverpool Edge Hill by-election in March 1979 with a swing against Labour of 32 per cent – one of the highest ever recorded in a by-election. (The seat is still held to this day by the Liberal David Alton.) A further electoral disaster was the failure to win the Liverpool seat for the European Parliament. Based on the projections of the general election results, this should have been one of Labour's safest seats. As it was, the result showed a swing of 21 per cent from what it should have been. Labour's candidate was a well-known Militant – Terry Harrison.

The final point I raised with the General Secretary concerned the sale of premises owned by the Tuebrook branch of Kirkdale Constituency Labour Party to Militant Newspapers for £6,500. Labour had held a great march and demonstration against unemployment in Liverpool at this time. I had taken part in this, but had arrived early in Liverpool so I could go and look at these premises. Consulting estate agents in the immediate area about local property values, I came to the conclusion that the suggested price of the premises was about half the current market value for the property. Somebody was getting a good deal, but it certainly wasn't the Labour Party. Although I reported this to the National Executive nothing was done and the sale went through.

Eventually an inquiry was set up by the Labour Party into Militant. It found that the Tendency was a well-organised centrally controlled caucus operating in the Party. Moreover, it was not a group 'formed solely to support a newspaper. It had a hard core of supporters (including its full-time employees) who form an organisation with its own programme and policy for distinctive and separate propaganda which is determined outside the structure of the Labour Party . . . ' The NEC recommended that there should be a register for pressure groups in the Party and that there should be no secret organisations. It also concluded that the Militant Tendency did not qualify. Benn and his supporters opposed the move to disqualify the Tendency. Action was taken against some of the leading members, but a great deal of damage had been done. This problem is still there and Militant continues its efforts in the Party. Militant is also active in the trade union movement. Wherever there is a lack of vigilance they will make inroads. These are the sorts of activities which should be borne in mind when considering the question of pressures to change the method of electing the Party Leader and reselection.

Militant found ready allies among others on the extreme left to join in its campaign of denunciation and denigration of the Parliamentary Party leadership. Many people in the Labour movement are fond of complaining of bias in the 'media', but even the most partisan newspapers appear as sucking-doves compared with some of the vitriolic abuse heaped upon the Labour leadership by alleged Party members and supporters. In their sayings and actions, these people never took any account of the precarious position of Labour when in Government. Rather than trying to give support to beleaguered Ministers and backbenchers, resolutions continued to pour in from the constituency parties demanding extreme action and constitutional change.

The constitution of the Party, adopted in 1918, had been drafted by people of goodwill, to be operated by people of goodwill. What was not foreseen was that the time would come when some of the goodwill would evaporate and that the constitution and its provisions would be used by people with ulterior motives. Who could possibly have foreseen that a time would arrive when young, mobile middle class people would be prepared to move from one address to another, simply to gain political control of a particular ward or constituency party. Militant supporters, in particular, are adept at this tactic.

My own Bristol South constituency was only one of many where this happened. Many of my Labour colleagues in the Commons reported the same thing. Some addresses became crowded with names on the electoral register. It should be remembered that urban Labour constituencies are particularly vulnerable to this movement because of the nature of the housing stock. This shifting of accommodation for political ends was particularly unfair on trade unionists and working class people. Apart from the fact that ordinary people would never even consider moving for political advantage, many trade unionists are restricted to where they can live by the position of their work place and the need to often work irregular hours.

Despite all this, despite the much greater difficulties for blue collar trade unionists to attend meetings, Wedgwood Benn and his associates still resist any change in the method of reselection in the name of fairness to trade unions. I have already mentioned the abuse which is frequently used to drive delegates away. For middle class people, often educated at university, to use their intellectual skills and training in articulacy and advocacy to browbeat, intimidate and ridicule working class people is nothing less than disgraceful behaviour. It is elitism of the worst sort. And yet many of these people are prominent in the 'Wedgwood Benn Fan Club'. He does not repudiate them.

There is also another aspect to this subversion of the Party's true aims of equality and social justice for ordinary people. For too long the Young Socialists have been tolerated when it was known that they had been taken over and completely dominated by Militant. This problem was typified by the row over the appointment of Andy Bevan as the national Youth Officer. An avowed Militant supporter, he was formerly a member of Benn's Bristol South-East constituency party. His appointment had been strongly resisted by the leadership of the Party, but eventually went through with Benn's backing.

Andy Bevan operated with some flair – for his and Militant's purposes. During the 1983 General Election campaign, for example, I was somewhat nonplussed to find that Michael Foot, the Party Leader, was appearing at election meetings for three out of the four known Militant Labour candidates. At the Labour Party headquarters one day during the election campaign, I passed the room where the meetings programmes were arranged. The person in charge was Andy Bevan.

A change of rule was smuggled through the Labour Party conference around this time. The effect of this was to remove the restriction which limited the number of Young Socialist branches and Women's Sections to one of each per constituency. The reasons given for this were matters such as the difficulties of travel. This may well have been true in rural constituencies but hardly applied to urban areas. And it was the extremists in the densely populated urban constituencies who took advantage of this change of rule, for one good reason. Each branch formed meant more delegates to the general management committee, thereby creating more chances for seizing control.

Thus in my own Bristol South constituency, a long-established Women's Section suddenly found that several other similar sections had grown up almost overnight. Each section sent delegates to the selection conference where I was to be deposed. Now they have all faded away again, except the original one. Similarly, a sudden bloom of Young Socialist branches in Bristol South has now been reduced to one again. At meetings of the South-West Regional Executive, I occasionally commented on the fact that the South-West of England's Young Socialist delegates were given to speak with a Liverpool accent.

During my time as Labour Chief Whip, I took a keen interest in the number of full-time Militant organisers that I could trace. Usually it was possible to obtain this information from colleagues and other sources. This information was obtained in the early 1980s. In comparison to the number of full-tine constituency Labour Party agents the results were astonishing:

Region	Full-time Labour Agents	Full-time Militant Organisers
Scotland	4	17
Northern	3	6
East Midlands	2	5
Eastern	25	2
North-West	4	18
West Midlands	1	21
Wales	2	11
South-West	1	2
South	4	10
North-East	2	9
Labour headquarters	130	
Militant headquarters		100

If there were any remaining doubts that Militant was acting as a 'party' within a party surely these figures are conclusive evidence. Otherwise, why should Militant have so many organisers on the ground. The high proportion of Labour Party agents in the Eastern region is a reflection of the close-knit nature of

135

the villages and small towns in this predominantly arable farming community.

The Militant strength in Scotland reflects the large number of seats in Scotland, which are 'up for grabs' if Militant can infiltrate effectively. On the other hand, the poor Militant showing in the Northern and North-East regions recognises the difficulty of them being able to penetrate what are traditional industrial Labour heartlands and which still provide a succession of basically moderate Labour MPs.

The Militant strength on Merseyside is self-evident, and correlates with what has been said about Liverpool. The strength in the West Midlands probably reflects Militant's new target of trying to infiltrate the trade unions. This is easier in an area like the West Midlands where there is a wide diversity of industry, particularly in light engineering. This contrasts somewhat with the East Midlands, where industry is not so concentrated and Labour seats fewer. There is some Militant activity in Wales, but it is mainly restricted to the major towns such as Cardiff and Swansea. Making any headway in the coalfields area is difficult, although some has been made. Both Labour and Militant strength in the South-West is a fair reflection of Labour's prospects in this area. It is now reduced to one Labour seat, my old Bristol South constituency with a Labour majority of 1,404. Similarly in the Southern region, although there is some activity at Brighton and Southampton. As for London, the poor Militant showing there reflects the numerous extremist groups with which Militant has to compete. Labour's figure for headquarters staff is not exceptional for a national political party. Nor is Militant's headquarters figure surprising, considering that they admitted to 50 full-time workers when they submitted their return to the Labour Party.

The accuracy of these Militant figures cannot be guaranteed, but they are near enough the mark to show the absurdity of Militant's claim that it is not a separate party within a party. And as long as the Labour Party fails to act on situations like this, so long will it be unable to convince the general public that it is not a party where there is extremism. The Labour leadership, and that means the National Executive, has got to come to realise that these people, and people like them, are only interested in a

Labour victory on their own terms. And these are terms which the British electorate will not stand at any price. The remedy lies in the Party's own hands. If the nettle is grasped, the Labour leadership will be astonished at the millions who will return to Labour once again. If they don't, then they are betraying the aspirations of these same millions and are not likely to be easily forgiven.

13

BRISTOL SOUTH – RETRIBUTION

The machinations that went on inside Bristol South constituency to unseat me as the Member of Parliament were not untypical of what was happening to many of my Labour MP colleagues up and down the country. Few activists would deny that they were supporters of Wedgwood Benn. Indeed, one of their aims was to put Bennite sympathisers in the seats of those they wanted to displace. As elsewhere, the activists in Bristol South were eager beavers who wanted to block off the channels of my support and create other conduits for their own kind. Having achieved this they could open the floodgates and swamp the reselection conference with their own votes.

Though some were known locally, they were not national figures whose identity and beliefs will be readily understood. But it is from such acorns that twisted oaks sometimes grow. In order to understand what occurred in Bristol South – not untypical, as I say, of the political rough trade and sharp practices applied in other constituencies – it is necessary to introduce some of those involved.

There was, for example, Dawn Primarolo, a former constituency secretary of Benn's old Bristol South-East constituency party, who was now a delegate to my Bristol South constituency party. She had already stood for the chairmanship of the constituency party when it was re-created out of the boundary redistribution and had been defeated. Dawn Primarolo was also at that time Chairman of the Bristol District

Party. She is now the Labour MP for Bristol South. Another was Ben Barker, a lecturer at Bristol South Technical College and also treasurer of the Bristol District Labour Party. He too had been a member of Benn's old constituency party but had transferred back into my constituency party. He was eventually to become constituency Chairman.

These are but two who were in the forefront of those wishing to impose their own brand of politics upon the constituency party, alienating traditional party supporters in the process.

There was a heavy tide running against Labour in the 1983 General Election. My own majority was reduced to 4,600 – the lowest I had ever had and I found myself the sole Labour MP in the South-West of England. The issues which told against us were defence, where we were still experiencing the backwash of the Falklands conflict and also divisions within the Labour Party itself. People simply will not put up with squabbling and wrangling – yet Labour never seems to learn.

If one looks at the opinion polls in the early 1980s, there were three substantial drops in Labour's support. The first slump in support came after the Wembley conference, already dealt with. The second drop occurred in the long summer campaign for the deputy leadership of the Party between Denis Healey, John Silkin and Wedgwood Benn in 1981. The general public certainly did not regard it as a 'healing process' as Benn claimed, and registered their disapproval accordingly. The third came after the Falklands conflict. This need not have been but, as explained earlier, I believe it was triggered off by the policy promoted by Wedgwood Benn and Judith Hart of wanting the task force to stop at the Equator once it had set sail. This policy enabled the Conservative Government to regain the initiative it was in danger of losing politically.

Immediately Benn had been selected for Bristol East I said that anybody from Bristol South who was anxious to help him both before and during the general election went with my encouragement. I did not mind at all since this was the sort of transfer of personnel and resources that I had originally been trying to encourage in my old Bristol West days.

However, it did give rise to an unpleasant incident in the Southville ward whose composition, as we have seen, was fairly

139

Bennite. Knowing that the Southville Party members would go to Bristol East to work, we arranged an organisation for polling day which did not involve that ward's members in any way. We obtained committee rooms in the houses of those who were helping me, some cars, and organised number takers at the polling stations. The latter is not unimportant for it is the taking of polling numbers that enables Party workers to go round 'knocking up' known Labour supporters later in the day. For this to be effective, of course, you must know where such supporters are. Without Southville's canvas returns from previous elections and their marked-up electoral register we could do nothing.

We never got them. Frequent requests were made but to no avail. I even rang up the Southville ward chairman and appealed to him to have the records produced for us. There was no response. On polling day itself I even went to Bristol East and met Benn to ask him if he could intervene with Southville to provide the records. He promised to do his best, but when the polls closed at 10 o'clock that evening we had not received one record from the ward. A complaint was later made to the regional office about this behaviour, but although sympathetically received, in reality there was little that could be done. However, it showed me and my supporters very clearly which way the wind was blowing. This wind was soon to turn into a gale.

Hopefully the reader going through this chapter will bear in mind that all the time this nonsense was going on in Bristol South I was Chief Whip of the Parliamentary Labour Party. It was a job that meant being in the House of Commons to all hours. A Chief Whip needs to be present until the end of business and, as we have seen, always present on Fridays when most MPs are away cultivating their constituencies. He also has to maintain the morale among Labour MPs, and try to help colleagues who may be having a difficult time. Moreover, he has to do his best to help work the Labour team into an effective Opposition. All this work did not cut much ice with the new wave of activists in Bristol South.

With the Bristol South electorate it was a different matter. I was constantly touched by the number of people who wrote to me with their problems and who included a phrase in their letters to the effect that 'I am sorry to bother you because I know how busy you are.'

There was no such understanding from my constituency's new activists. I was also unpopular with them because I had very strong views on an MP's right to exercise his conscience in voting on matters such as civil liberties, abortion and similar issues. While I had, in their eyes, one of the most reactionary voting records on these issues, much of this was because of votes I had cast bearing in mind my position as Chief Whip. It was a factor the activists chose to ignore, and my voting record was all grist to the mill for those who wished me no good fortune.

Evidence continued to accumulate of the moves against me. When two local district councillors from Bristol South, vice-chairmen of my constituency party, were nominated for the panel of municipal candidates they were both turned down after interview by the Bristol District Labour Party. They were two out of only four applicants who were turned down, a coincidence which was too much for me to stomach. Both men appealed to the Party's regional office and eventually one was accepted and the other rejected. When I mentioned this absurd situation to members of the National Executive Committee, they made a change in the constitution whereby, when it came to reselection for local elections, a sitting Labour councillor automatically has the right to be on the short list of candidates for the ward he represents. It was a change that did not endear me to the 'hard-left' in Bristol South.

This was not the first time I had suspected the Bristol District Labour Party was interfering in Bristol South affairs. In June 1982, I had written to the South-West Regional Organiser pointing out that when I had been Chairman of the Bristol Borough Labour Party some twenty years before, people were not forever rushing to the rule book and the constitution. 'There is now bitterness among some recently joined members of the Labour movement in Bristol towards loyal, long-serving comrades that I have not experienced before,' I said. 'Now that the District Labour Party annual general meeting is over, I must tell you that I am extremely disturbed over the way my own Bristol South AGM was declared invalid,' I said. It was a

141

complicated business which need not detain us here, but sufficient to state that my complaint was justified. If evidence is needed of the attitude of the District Labour Party towards the Bristol South constituency, there was the calculated removal of its secretary, Christine Wilkins, a position she had held since 1976, and who was a strong supporter of mine. All sorts of stratagems were applied, including challenges as to whether certain members present were eligible to vote. The instigators were Dawn Primarolo, Chairman of the District Party and Ben Barker, the District treasurer. It was at this meeting that Barker succeeded in defeating one of my supporters as chairman and Christine Wilkins was declared ineligible to stand as secretary. The allegations about ineligibility to vote at the meeting is not without its importance, for more reasons than one. Primarolo's case was that some of the unions had not paid their affiliation fees and therefore their delegates could not vote.

She was supported in this by Barker, who presented the District Party's financial accounts. Both of them were officers of the District Party, though it should be stressed that it was as constituency party delegates they were attending the meeting. Moreover, at this time, no other Bristol Labour constituency party was being challenged by officers of the District Labour Party over the delegates attending its meetings. In other words, Bristol South was being singled out for special treatment. Primarolo said that the accounts were in order, having been audited. In fact they had not. Her objections to some of those present were upheld. Six of the delegates left the meeting, to be followed by others too disgusted at what was going on. Though the voting that took place was later challenged – the objections even going to the national headquarters – the anti-Cocks brigade were to get their way at a subsequent reconvened annual meeting. The Left, in the end, were to make a clean sweep of all the important offices in the constituency party.

There are other instances on record which would perhaps sound too parochial to document here but, none the less, had a direct bearing on what influences were being brought to bear upon the constituency and the pressures that were being applied to those who supported me. At one time the Party's National Executive had to set up an inquiry into the irregularities alleged at annual meetings. Though the inquiry team declared that the AGM in March 1984 was invalid, it was now, a year on, too late to do anything about it. They advised that the best way forward was to properly convene and conduct the 1985 AGM as soon as possible.

This took place in July and the Left tightened its grip. As the *Bristol Evening Post* reported: 'Last year, majorities had been in single figures; last night the gap was 25 to 30 votes out of 130.' This did not reflect growing ward membership, but rather the effort to pile on more and more delegates for the forthcoming reselection battle. There was an increase in delegates from the women's sections, all but one of which have now closed down. There was also a predominance of delegates from the Bennite Southville and Windmill Hill wards. Moreover, 48 delegates in the total of 151 came from the area which was part of Benn's old Bristol South-East constituency.

Some may ask why counter recruitment was not done. The answer is that it was, but the efforts eventually ran out of steam. The reasons have been explained previously: if things seem to be slipping from the 'hard-left's' grasp, the old tactics of rudeness, points of order, and time-wasting are resorted to. The plain truth is that many ordinary folk simply will not put up with this sort of treatment. They have better things to do and more valuable ways of spending their time. Furthermore, once the position of secretary has gone, recovery is very much more difficult. That is why Christine Wilkins was displaced. Whitchurch Park ward, for example, had been captured by my opponents. The delegates had shifted from the working class estate centred on the Labour Club to the middle class private housing estate which I inherited from Wedgwood Benn's old Bristol South-East constituency on redistribution.

I have been criticised for the intransigence of my stance and my unwillingness to bend in these circumstances. Maybe I should have taken the easy way out and cooperated after the takeover by the Left. But I did not have only myself to consider. During my time as Chief Whip, I had seen dozens of my colleagues in the House of Commons subjected to similar treatment. Some of them decided to stay on and fight, some almost cracked under the strain, while others gave up and retired. Now it was my turn. If the Left were prepared to do this to the Chief Whip of the Labour Party and got away with it unscathed – then what hope was there for other Labour MPs who were not lucky enough to hold the sort of position that I had?

One senior colleague came to see me after he had visited Bristol. He said he had tested the water and my opponents were anxious to build bridges towards me. I replied that I was not prepared to give an inch and outlined some of the things that had gone on. He went on to say that it would be a catastrophe if the Chief Whip of the Party was deselected. Replying I said that he should have thought of that before, when he supported the whole absurd proposal of mandatory reselection. 'What have you left if you lose your seat?' he asked. I replied that I didn't want to sound pious but at least I would have my self-respect.

My own reselection process began in the autumn of 1985. Such are the cannibalistic instincts engendered by this process that my wife, who was secretary of the Filwood ward, even received applications from people asking to be nominated by the Filwood ward against her own husband! One hopeful wrote: 'I very much hope that there will be selection conferences in the usual way and if there are, would like to be considered for these please.' This refers to the practice of wards and trade union branches holding their own meeting with several hopefuls to choose which of them they will nominate for the main selection meeting. A moment's thought will show that a sitting MP is at a great disadvantage here. Either he has to leave his duties at Westminster to appear at all these preselection meetings or malcontents can further undermine him by suggesting that he is not interested if he does not appear. This is not simply an individual choice for the sitting MP; the Labour Chief Whip has the problem of maintaining an effective force in the House of Commons while faced with a barrage of requests from MPs for absence for these reasons.

In case it is thought I am exaggerating over the character assassination that can take place, let me give one example. Several years ago I had a varicose vein operation. I was told to keep my legs raised whenever possible for several weeks afterwards. One day I chanced across a delegation in the House of Commons who had come from the Bristol area to lobby against possible closure of a local hospital. I found a room for them and listened to their case, promising to do what I could and offering to contact their local MP. At the start of the meeting I explained about my legs and put them on the table. Later I heard that on returning to Bristol, one of the lobbyists had put it about that I was so bored and uninterested when they were seeing me that I had my feet on the table all the time!

There is no need to linger too long over my own reselection process. After nominations in Bristol South had been called for, a meeting was held on 9 January 1986 to prepare a short list. There were nine nominations, including my own. This may not seem very many for what is a 'plum' Labour seat. However, I know of at least three former Labour MPs who had lost their seats who were approached to see if they would accept nomination in Bristol South. Each refused point blank saying they would not be party to taking a former colleague's job off him. Two of these were not having an easy time economically either. It is difficult for Labour MPs who lose their seats to find other work. There are far too many inbuilt prejudices among employers to give them a fair chance. My former colleagues' refusals were based on that old fashioned quality of loyalty which today is in rather short supply in some quarters.

A short list of five came out of this meeting. One local candidate was wrongly eliminated in the voting procedure which later led to complaints to Labour national headquarters, but nothing was done. In fact what happened was not only incorrect, but grossly unfair, and in itself sufficient to invalidate the proceedings. The five who went forward were John Aitkin, an electrician from Essex, Andrew May, the Southville councillor whom we have encountered before, Dawn Primarolo, again already mentioned, Pam Tatlow, a local councillor, and myself.

The selection conference was held on a Sunday afternoon, 19 January, at Merrywood Boys' School. The winner was chosen by exhaustive ballot. On the first ballot I polled 55 votes. One candidate was eliminated on each ballot until I went into the fourth and final ballot against Dawn Primarolo. She won by 71 votes to 56. In other words, I had added only one vote in four ballots, such was the determination to get rid of me. As I have said before, no complaints were raised against me over my work either in Bristol or at Westminster. But I knew the way things would turn out after beating Benn for the new Bristol South seat. Possibly I might have been allowed one more Parliament if I had been prepared to trim and compromise, but it simply wasn't worth it.

I had met Ben Barker during the 1983 General Election when I had been out with the loudspeaker electioneering in Upton Road, Southville. He was collecting Labour Party subscriptions. Barker said that he wanted to have a talk with me after the election. I said certainly, but pointed out that I had heard him say at a previous Labour Party meeting that we all had to work together. I went on to say that working together was obviously better, but we didn't have to work together, and he could have it whichever way he wanted. When he got up at the Annual General Meeting on 2 February, to support Dawn Primarolo's challenge to the delegates, I knew that he had made his choice.

At the time I was deselected the size of my general management committee was the second largest in the country. Afterwards, when the job had been done, it shrank rapidly – a common phenomenon in these cases which I christened 'post-deselection detumescence'. To be truthful, if some of the people who voted against me had voted for me instead I would have felt unclean. I had not shifted from the view expressed by myself and other Bristol people during the deputy leadership campaign of 1981: that it would be a disaster if Wedgwood Benn became deputy leader or leader of the Labour Party. If losing my own seat in the House of Commons was the price that had to be paid to prevent this, then it was a price that I was only too willing to pay.

14

CHESTERFIELD

There was no doubt as to the fury of the Bennites in Bristol after he lost his Bristol East seat in 1983. One illustration will suffice, but it is indicative of how they felt. My wife attended a conference shortly after the defeat when Dawn Primarolo and another Benn supporter came over and hissed at her. She recalls: 'They said it was my fault that Tony Benn was not the Prime Minister of the country. I said they were "nuts", to which they replied, "Well, perhaps not your fault but your husband's". I asked them what they were talking about. We had lost the General Election and Tony Benn didn't even get his seat and got the following reply: "It was because Mike Cocks didn't give Tony Bristol South that Tony lost Bristol East because it was a marginal".'

But what was to become of Benn? I was an unknowing instrument in his next move. In November 1983, I had to attend the memorial meeting for Alan Mason, the former South-West Regional Organiser of the Labour Party. He had been a staunch full-time officer of the Party for many years. He was a very old friend of mine and I was asked to give an address at the meeting held for him at Transport House, Bristol. Wedgwood Benn, who, as we saw, was no longer an MP, had also been asked to speak. Coming out of Temple Meads station on arrival in Bristol, I met Benn who had travelled from London on the same train. I thanked him for writing to me congratulating me on my re-election as Chief Whip. He seemed puzzled and said he did not recall having written. I assured him he had and said I would show him the letter when we got to Transport House for the meeting. I then casually mentioned that I had just heard from Eric Varley – his successor as Industry Secretary when Benn had been moved to the Department of Energy – to say he was taking a job with Coalite and would be leaving the Commons. Eric Varley was MP for Chesterfield and his decision would mean a by-election. Thus it was that I gave Benn a flying start in his efforts to obtain the nomination as Labour candidate and with it an almost assured ticket back to the House of Commons. As for that letter, when I showed it to Benn I realised it was from Tony Berry, Conservative MP for Southgate and a Government Whip, who was to be tragically killed in the Brighton bomb outrage at the Conservative Party conference in 1984. We had been great friends.

Thus, ironically, I was instrumental in giving Wedgwood Benn his head start in his efforts to return to Parliament. In the ensuing by-election he beat off a large number of other contesttants and was elected to take his seat in the Commons on 6 March, 1984. It meant that within a year of losing his seat in Bristol East he was an MP again, this time for the important mining and engineering seat of Chesterfield.

Within a week of taking his seat, the trouble which had been brewing in the coal mining industry for some time finally erupted. The strike started on 13 March and was to last almost twelve months. It cost 26.1 million working days, quite apart from all the hardships suffered by the miners and their families. Naturally, from the start Benn was closely involved in the dispute. Any MP for Chesterfield would have been. But, of course, in this case the newly elected Member was a politician of some thirty-five years' experience. He was able to bring to bear all his extensive knowledge of procedure and propaganda.

Within two days of the strike starting he waded into the Home Secretary, Leon Brittan, over the question of picketing of collieries:

'Is the right hon. Gentleman aware of the charge being made against him – that, having employed Mr McGregor

148

to destroy the right to work in the steel industry, having destroyed the right of those in Cheltenham [the GCHQ intelligence gathering establishment] to vote on trade union membership, and now having released Mr MacGregor to destroy the right to work of 20,000 miners, what he said was insensitive, provocative, odious and hypocritical and that he should accept responsibility for everything that is happening in the coalfields?'

It was a meaty contribution. On the same day, Benn raised the question of the occupation of the Speedwell Rooms in Chesterfield and the Ashgate Hospital, and asked for a categorical assurance from the Government that the armed forces had not been put on the alert. On 28 March he applied for an emergency debate to discuss police conduct during the dispute. It was only one of many attempts to force the issue of the dispute into debate on the floor of the House of Commons. In a debate on 10 April, Benn made a powerful speech including accusations of telephone tapping and the deliberate slowing down of the processing of applications for benefits to put financial pressure on the miners and their families. Benn pursued the Government throughout that summer and in the November he spoke vigorously on the Miners Families (Benefits) Order:

'I warn the House – I do so because I believe that to be one of the functions of an elected Member – that unless justice is given this battle will continue, with increasing bitterness and horror. The responsibility rests with those who began it with the pit closure programme. Today's mean and vicious little order, which we would not have debated without the action taken by some hon. Members, is only one of many attacks on the living standards of the finest group of workers in Britain – those who labour underground to give the country access to coal, our one natural resource in plenty, and upon which our future is founded.'

Wedgwood Benn kept up his battle on behalf of the miners into the following year. Meanwhile, however, the Wapping printing dispute had flared up. Once more there were scenes on television of clashes between demonstrators and the police. Benn was quick to draw a parallel with the mining dispute. Because of these disputes his interest in security matters quickened even further. He interested himself in questions on the Birmingham bombers – said by Chris Mullin, now an MP, to have been wrongly convicted – the Special Branch and, latterly, the row over the publication of Peter Wright's book *Spycatcher*.

Unfortunately, both the mining and Wapping disputes were used by extremist groups to create disturbances and cause scenes of disorder which, when shown on television, caused a growing loss of sympathy for the causes they were purporting to support. Their motivations were the same as those who have infiltrated the Labour movement: to destabilise society and reduce the credibility of the Labour Party as an alternative government, thus paving the way for revolution. Such objectives, of course, are fantasies, the addled aims of blinkered zealots who do not know the nature of the British people. And some of those fomenting trouble at industrial disputes are the same well-educated people who have infiltrated the Labour Party and consciously driven away working class supporters from meetings by sneering laughter and downright abuse. Working class people will not put up with this treatment and cease to attend. Hence the extremists' influence is strengthened until they dominate.

Wedgwood Benn himself has said that unlike many others who have become more right wing as they get older, his experience has driven him towards the left. His antipathy to the House of Lords is well-known, but where he is at his weakest is in fostering the myths about the all-pervading influence of the Civil Service and their power. His message is that civil servants are the obstacles to reform, that they are the watchdogs of the status quo, particularly when a Labour Government is in office. It is not like that at all. Before a general election the Civil Service look through the parties' manifestos and begin contingency plans to implement them while the election is in progress. Once over, the framework of the winner's programme, at least, is already prepared. In other words, if a minister is run by the civil servants it is nobody's fault but his own. Aneurin Bevan once said that within 48 hours of a minister taking office, the civil servants know whether he is going to run the department or whether they are going to have to carry it for him. Benn should know better than lay blame where it does not reside, but presumably he finds it in his own interests to foment discontent by criticising the Civil Service, especially as they keep a low profile and cannot answer back.

Benn's own self-analysis of his shifting position is over-simplified. Rather he has made a transition from one who held some of the highest offices of the State, with all the responsibilities that that entails, to someone who has become a rather crude propagandist. Anybody with Benn's wealth of parliamentary experience would know perfectly well that the great clutch of Bills he presented in the Commons had not the slightest chance of becoming law by his chosen method. I mention some of them: Crown Prerogatives (House of Commons Control), Local Authorities (General Powers), Northern Ireland (Termination of Jurisdiction), Foreign Nuclear, Chemical and Biological Bases (Prohibition), Miners' Amnesty Bill. Such knowledge of the parliamentary system is by no means universal and many would not understand why no progress could be made. Moreover, some who did realise the unreality of expecting progress would conceal this information from others and instead use the Bills as sticks with which to berate and attack the Labour leadership for inaction, lack of interest and all the other tired old shibboleths which are trotted out at times like these. It is quite true that this is a good way of getting issues raised and talked about. But it is never made clear that this is the purpose. Over this matter Benn has been less than straightforward.

Where I do think he carries a great burden of responsibility is in some of the statements made about former Labour Governments, Labour leaders and Labour MPs. Anyone is entitled to change their mind on great issues as Benn did on the Common Market and on nuclear power. But what is the general public to make of a political party which in office does one thing and then, when out of government, some of its prominent figures begin to berate and belittle its efforts? If I do have a bee in my bonnet, it is for those bigots who build barricades against a rational examination of what Labour Governments have and have not done. Benn is to blame because by his actions he has created an arsenal of half-truths, to be used by his supporters at random. At Labour Party conferences, when the ground was being prepared for the push to change the Party's constitution, they fired these bullets of abuse with such indiscrimination at Labour MPs that at one time I thought of pressing to have them made a protected species. Much of this virulent denigration, of course, came from the Militant Tendency who had nothing but their own objectives in view.

When Benn was running for the leadership in 1976, he issued two statements about his candidature and circulated them to MPs. In his covering letter he said: 'I strongly support the manifestos on which we fought the 1974 elections.' Yet when interviewed in *The Independent* in March 1987 he had this to say: ' . . . actually the SDP has been in power in Britain since 1945, Churchill and Attlee were SDP in terms of the policies they pursued.' How does one equate this with his call in December 1977, as reported in the *Western Daily Press*: 'Mr Benn said in London last night the pioneering spirit of the post-war Government should inspire Labour's next election manifesto. "Then the Party won overwhelming national support for policies which committed us to full employment by planning, public investment and public ownership; and to a greatly expanded Welfare State. We must offer real vision backed by workmanlike plans as Clem Attlee called them to climb out of the recession".'

The Labour Party has enough enemies without this heavy criticism and expedient re-writing of history within its own ranks. Benn's attitude towards the press and broadcasters has also hardened. We have seen how he constantly supported the independence of the broadcasting authorities during his time as Postmaster General – but free from the responsibility of office his attitude has changed. Indeed, Christopher Mayhew, a former Labour MP and minister who joined the Liberals, said in his book *Time to Explain* that the last straw for him which led him to leave the Labour Party were some proposals put to Labour's National Executive by Benn for the control of public broadcasting.

Working people know that newspapers propagate particular political views, and despite the sneers of the new intellectuals, they have more than enough sense to recognise and allow for this. I can give a graphic illustration of this from my own former Bristol South constituency. At my counts on polling day I used to sample – as happens in every other constituency – the random bundles of fifty votes as they were being checked. In my strongest area, in a good election, I would get 43, 44 or 45 in each 50. It so happened I used to be friendly with a newsagent in that area and would sometimes help him unpack and lay out the day's papers. He sold more copies of the *Sun* – not exactly Labour's best friend – than all the other newspapers put together.

Ordinary working people are not stupid. They read papers like the *Sun* for reasons other than the political comment. But what they do not understand and what makes a deep impact upon them is when well-known and respected Labour Party members denigrate Labour leaders and the achievements of Labour Governments, thereby handing out fodder to the politically hostile newspapers.

What people want is a political party that they can trust – not run by politicians who have been working in a team to run the country and then start running each other down when out of office. If they can trust the party and feel that the leaders trust each other then, that is good enough. But once confidence is broken it cannot be easily regained.

After the 1979 General Election when Labour lost office, a campaign began to disparage the Labour Government's efforts to implement its manifesto pledges. This was certainly an orchestrated part of the campaign to change the way in which the manifesto was prepared. I produced a list of Labour's 1974 election promises and how many had been implemented. It showed that the vast majority of Labour's promises had been carried out – and this despite, as was previously described, the loss of Labour's majority in Parliament. This checklist was published on the centre pages of the now defunct *Labour Weekly*. I suggested to the National Executive that a poster be printed showing the percentage of our election promises carried out. It was a suggestion that did not go down well with the left-wing members who were pressing for constitutional changes and was never implemented.

There are two great traps into which politicians can fall. The first is to begin to believe their own propaganda, and the other is to arouse expectations in people which cannot be fulfilled. The first is an unconscious thing that afflicts most politicians from time to time. Usually when it is pointed out to the person it is realised and there is no harm done. But when the belief becomes obsessional it is dangerous. The arousing of expectations is another matter. Usually this is done deliberately. It is known that targets are being put forward which are unrealistic. It is both a cruel and dangerous exercise. Firstly, it manipulates the natural feelings of folk anxious to have wrongs righted and conditions improved. Secondly, and much more insidiously, it undermines the democratic process. Because issues are presented in such simplistic terms, as with the Bills previously mentioned, hopes are raised which cannot be satisfied. The inevitable frustration this engenders reflects discredit on the parliamentary or council system which seems unable to deliver the goods.

Thus Benn gathered around him, unconsciously no doubt, although he should have seen with his experience what was happening, a group of left-wing extremists. They are people who know they have no chance of attempting to create a revolutionary situation in this country as long as there is a strong and viable Labour alternative to the Conservative Government. Their constant sniping and denigration within the Party, therefore, has eroded the trust which voters once had in Labour. And the people who have suffered as a result have been the deprived, the disabled and others who looked to Labour as the natural haven for their support.

Over the last few years a number of people have said to me that Wedgwood Benn has done immense damage to the Party. If this is so, I do not think it is because of the shifts in his attitudes to issues which have taken place over the years. Rather, it is that he has allowed himself to be used by an army of people, many of whom basically do not want the Party to succeed. Benn has used his immense gifts to destroy confidence in Labour through his onslaught upon its constitution when he could so

154

easily have used those talents to be entirely constructive.

I believe that this has occurred because of the rarefied atmosphere in which he operated from childhood. Pure politics is bad for one, just as premature babies can be damaged by too much oxygen. He should have recognised that those elderly people in Bristol South-East were the heart and soul of the Party, not the new influx of variously motivated intellectuals. It is the former who would have been sufficient to save him from the grosser errors he made in later years. In the final analysis, Wedgwood Benn has done a great disservice to the Labour movement. Without his acknowledged powers of oratory and persuasion, I have little doubt that the divisive campaigns on the major constitutional issues of mandatory reselection and changing the method of electing the Labour leader – campaigns which he aided and abetted – would never have developed their great, and, in the end, damaging impetus. Nor can there be any doubt about the effect these issues had on Labour's chances of regaining power. As such, Benn has had an influence on recent political history shared by few others.

These final pages are being penned with another Labour conference well behind us. Once again Benn's leadership challenge has been defeated. Now let us be done with these divisive contests. We should be creating a forum for the discussion of ideas instead of creating a smoke screen behind which the Conservative Government continues to carry out its drastic policies – policies that are harmful to the very people whom we need to reclaim as our supporters.

The Labour Party must look forward. Organisationally things can be done to improve the Party machinery, but this will be like polishing the brass on the *Titanic* if there is not a coming together in fellowship with the aim of a united trust to gain power at the next general election. The same opportunity presents itself for Labour now as I mentioned when I spoke to the Young Socialists on Westbury Downs in 1959. This time, however, instead of having the contrasts within Britain which were labelled 'private affluence, public squalor', the whole problem has shifted onto a global scale.

The planning and use of public resources is now needed worldwide. The exploitation of the environment since the first

Industrial Revolution has so raped the earth that many scientists now believe that unless immediate steps are taken the actual existence of the human race is in jeopardy. Natural disasters can no longer be attributed solely to acts of God; rather they are the acts of man. Recent floods in Bangladesh are due to the stripping of forest covers from river catchment areas. The rape of the Amazon rain forest is destroying one of the Earth's great lungs. The estimates of the effects of the build up of carbon dioxide in the atmosphere (better known as the greenhouse effect) become increasingly pessimistic. Sooner rather than later the burning of fossil fuel must come to a stop. This will create tensions in the countries of the Third World, who will criticise the developed nations for lecturing about not using the self-same fuels and materials which made them prosperous.

They are difficult problems. If only Wedgwood Benn would turn his talents to these instead of worrying about whether there should be a 'rolling manifesto' or, if Labour Cabinet ministers should be elected to office by the whole of the Party, he would be doing not only the Labour Party, but Britain and the world, a great favour. But, as we can see from his record, the prospects of a change of attitude are remote. He has become the unfortunate victim of his own misguided propaganda.

APPENDIX I

Speech by the Rt. Hon. Anthony Wedgwood Benn, MP, at the Labour Party Annual Conference 1980, winding up for the National Executive Committee on the proposals to change the way in which the Labour Party prepared its manifesto for a general election.

'I do not think, that after hearing the last debate and hearing this one – and no doubt it will be the same in the next debate – anybody can doubt that, when we talk about the structure and democracy of our Party, we are talking about the life blood of democracy and we are not engaged in arid constitutional wrangles. We are really talking now, whatever view we take – and we do not all agree – about what it is that gives the Labour Party its moral strength that it believes that power should be shared and not concentrated at the top.

And the manifesto is the buckle that links this Conference with the policy of a Labour Government. (I do not believe that the Labour Party is only an electoral organisation. It is more than that, it is a campaigning organisation;) it is an educational organisation; it is an organisation designed to change people's perception and not just change their local and national represen-tatives. But it is also an organisation which exists to give the British people the chance to hear the case for Labour and, if they like it, to endorse it and to give it parliamentary majorities for one Parliament only at a time so that those changes can be carried through.

In my heart I am a Chartist. I really believe the annual Parlia-ment – the one unrealised Chartist demand – has got merit because the more you bring people into the discussion of their

157

parliamentary affairs, the better. But Clause V of the constitution is the means by which historically the Party has drawn up the manifesto. That is to say, the National Executive Committee (NEC) and the Parliamentary Committee of the PLP (Parliamentary Labour Party) draw it up. The NEC – if I come back to David Warburton – is overwhelmingly elected by the trade union section of the Party: 12 trade unionists: five women's section, of which the trade union vote is the majority; and the Treasurer himself. The National Executive has 18 out of its 28 members elected by the trade unions, and those who attack the Executive are attacking the trade union movement. [Applause]. May I put to Conference something that may not be fully appreciated. And I say this, having been at five – no, six – Clause V meetings. I was at the Clause V meeting that drew up the 1964, 66, 70, 74 and 79 manifestoes. First of all, when Labour is in power there is no Parliamentary Committee of the Parliamentary Party. When the manifesto in May of last year was drawn up not a single person there, except in the capacity of Leader and Deputy Leader, had been elected by the Parliamentary Party. It was an appointed, hand-picked Cabinet who represented Labour Members of Parliament. Let that be understood.

And I might carry it on: there was not a single Labour backbencher who saw that draft before it was approved by the Clause V meeting. So do not think that the present provision provides for backbench Members to see the manifesto; they have never seen it. They have never seen the text, either when we are in Opposition or when we are in Government and it is this proposal – and I will come to the details later – that for the first time will give trades unions and the Parliamentary Labour Party the right to see the text.

I will say more to David Warburton. His union has never seen the text of a draft manifesto before it was agreed, and neither has the Transport and General Workers' Union or the Amalgamated Union of Engineering Workers, because up to now it has been left to the National Executive Committee and the Cabinet or the Shadow Cabinet.

There is another snag about it. It is all drawn up so late that the country never knows what the Labour Government will do until three weeks before the campaign is carried out. [Applause].

And I must say this frankly, I profoundly believe that the only socialism we can achieve is by consent. But I also believe you cannot win consent in three weeks of a parliamentary election when nobody has been allowed to know with any authority what we would do when we came to power. [Applause].

And last of all – and I do not want to make too much of it – there is a veto which has crept in where a succession of Parliamentary Labour leaders have said "I will not have it. It must not appear." And I make not too much of that save for one thing. If you have a veto, those who oppose policies do not bother to argue with Conference, because they wait till the Clause V meeting and kill it secretly, privately, without debate. [Applause]. My resentment about the exclusion of the House of Lords – and you must not think I have any particular interest in that place – was not just that it was vetoed, but that when Conference discussed it and decided it by an overwhelming majority, no voice was raised from the platform to persuade us to drop it. They let the Conference pass it and it was vetoed secretly, late, quietly, before the Party could discover what had happened. That is wrong, and it is out of that that the mistrust in our Party grows.

But Jim (Callaghan) was right yesterday. No constitutional provision can be a substitute for confidence. But may I say – as one delegate said, who gave us a rather scholarly but wise lecture about responsibility and power – what I fear is this: that if Conference is denied power, it will pass irresponsible resolutions, knowing they will never be implemented. And then the parliamentary leadership may say, "Look at those irresponsible resolutions. We are not obliged to implement them." We have got to accept that this Conference must be given the power that goes with responsibility, and the whole movement in the country a chance to know how it should be handled.

Now I say one or two relevant matters, because I am more concerned with the future than I am with the past. Is there anybody in this Conference today who believes that, with our present Parliamentary Committee, there would in the next election be a commitment to withdraw from the Common Market in line with the two-thirds majority that was agreed this morning? It would not. It would be vetoed. Of course it would

159

be vetoed. And we would be irresponsible if we allowed resolutions like that to be passed and then allowed the power to rest where it does rest, where the power of veto would be exercised.

I come back to the GMWU. David, I have looked at your resolution. Every one of the points that was moved by David Basnett on Monday was put by the National Executive at the Clause V meeting and was ruled out. Eighteen months ago. Immediate restriction of the export of capital – ruled out. Reflation of public sector service spending – ruled out. Substantial cuts in arms expenditure – ruled out. The immediate introduction of a wealth tax – ruled out. [Applause]. The imposition of selected import controls – ruled out. I say there is no body of opinion at this Conference that has a greater vested interest in carrying the Executive's constitutional amendment than the trade union leaders and the trade union movement. [Applause].

For it is all very well – if I turn now, so as not to be seeming personal, to my own General Secretary, Moss [Evans, of the TGWU] – there is no point in coming in with a big block vote – and I am one of it – and demanding policies, and then using the same block vote in such a way as to permit the policies you demand to be vetoed by Parliamentarians who are not accountable to this Conference. [Applause].

I finish by saying two things. Alex Lyons said the first. The route to unity in this Party is not to lecture it to stop squabbling, but to start listening to the debate, to discuss the policy in advance of the moment, and to go on discussing it year after year after year. Then, when the movement has discussed, as we intend it should, the draft manifesto – to have gone through it four conferences running; to have listened to the Parliamentary Party; to have listened to the trade unions; to have let Women's Conference discuss it; to have let every regional and constituency party discuss it; then to take a decision and put it before the British people. That is the route to unity, and in that unity we only ask that the majority decisions accepted be as the policy of the Party, while everyone retains the right we must all have to continue to argue about what it should be next year.

But it is more than that. This is the route to popular support, because how can the public support a Labour Government if they are not allowed to know what we are going to do until the cacophony of the election campaign has begun? Do you imagine the press will give a fair share to Labour policy when polling day has been announced? Is it possible to get the manifesto out on to the doorsteps and through the letterboxes in the last three weeks? We say this – and that is what we invite you to do: to support the amendment; to look at this document, our draft manifesto, which is not for endorsement this week but is based upon past decisions; to discuss it in the unions, in the CLPs, in the PLP, the women's movement, among Young Socialists; and come back next year and do another draft manifesto. And then the public will hear the debate and know in advance – and I might add, even members of the public who are not members of the Labour Party will be able to influence the outcome, because they too, (can join in the debate), though the decision must rest with Conference.

I have made the best case I can. I genuinely believe, as Chairman of the Home Policy Committee – and if I speak with passion it is because I have been responsible now for five years – and I have seen policies develop in the sub-committees, come to the Executive, (go to the unions for consultation, be discussed in the Liaison Committee with the unions, come to Conference,) be endorsed, then I have seen them cast aside in secret by those who are not accountable to the movement. I invite you to support this amendment.' [Applause].

Appendix II

Speech by the Rt. Hon. Michael Cocks MP, on 7 June, 1981, at the General and Municipal Workers' Union Congress at Brighton.

'I particularly welcome and indeed sought the opportunity of addressing you today. The Chief Whip, probably more than anyone in the Party, is concerned over the issue of Party unity. This is the first time that I have ever spoken about my work in public because the tradition has been for the Chief Whip to maintain a low profile. I do not break from my normal practice lightly. I do so because I have been appalled at the misrepresentation of the work of the last Labour Government and the mischievous way that some have sought to use their misrepresentations to cause division in the Party. I would like to take this chance to put the record straight. In October 1974 Labour was elected with a majority of three; I would remind you this is the same majority that Labour went to the country with in 1951. Despite great difficulties, we immediately helped the trade unions:

The Labour Government passed:
* the 1974 Trade Union and Labour Relations Act (which included the repeal of the hated Industrial Relations Act of 1971);
* the 1974 Health and Safety at Work Act;
* in 1975 the Employment Protection Act;
* and in 1976 the Trade Union Labour Relations Amendment Act.

Our position in Parliament was gradually eroded and when I became Chief Whip in April 1976 I knew that the time when we could carry Socialist legislation on Labour votes alone was rapidly drawing to a close. In the autumn of 1976 we got through five great socialist measures on Aircraft and Shipbuilding nationalisation; Dock Work Regulation; National Health Service Pay Beds; the Education Act and the Abolition of Tied Cottages, and one of the greatest unsung acts of the last Labour Government, we effectively took control of our North Sea oil assets by the passing of the British North Sea Oil Corporation Act (BNOC). Here we took on the multi-national oil companies and succeeded in establishing a Public Ownership. But from this time onwards we had to depend on the support of various minorities and in due course this was formalised in our agreement with the Liberal Party.

Some now say with hindsight that we should have gone to the country for a general election but I must tell you this was not said at the time, indeed, many members of this union personally urged me to keep up the fight and not give in – when one looks at the shambles of the British economy today under the Tories, can anybody say we were wrong? Anybody who did not go through the ordeal, night after night, day after day, of maintaining a majority in the House can have no conception of the strain which it placed on Labour Members of Parliament and I have to tell you that because of the demands which I made on my Members, some of them laid down their lives for the Labour Movement as surely as if they had been shot in battle.

The last Labour Government has been accused of not carrying out the Manifesto on which it was elected. This is not true; don't take my word for it – get hold of the Manifesto checklist which was issued in *Labour Weekly* at the last election and see for yourselves just how much of the Manifesto was put through despite the difficulties I have already mentioned; the only major policy in the Manifesto which we failed to deliver was devolution, on which the Government was brought down.

I now turn to another great myth which has been fostered in an attempt to discredit the Labour leadership, the use of the veto in the preparation of the last Manifesto. This was referred to by Tony Benn, one of the candidates for the Deputy Leadership, who said that the Deputy Leadership election is about honesty, integrity and credibility. At last October's Conference he was winding up on the Manifesto debate for the National Executive when there was no chance of any reply from the floor and he dealt specifically with the resolution submitted by this union. He said, and I quote:

> "I come back to the GMWU. David [Warburton], I have looked at your resolution. Every one of the points that was moved by David Basnett on Monday was put by the National Executive at the Clause V meeting and was ruled out. Eighteen months ago. Immediate restriction of the export of capital – ruled out. Reflation of public sector service spending – ruled out. Substantial cuts in arms expenditure – ruled out. The immediate introduction of a wealth tax – ruled out. The imposition of selected import controls – ruled out. I say there is no body of opinion at this Conference that has a greater vested interest in carrying the Executive's constitutional amendment than the trade union leaders and the trade union movement."

Let us look at the five GMWU policies said by Tony Benn to have been ruled out of the 1979 Manifesto.

1. Immediate restriction of the export of capital – ruled out? *Wrong! The Labour Party Manifesto said, "A Labour Government will retain the power to impose import controls on capital movements."* (Page 33.)
2. Reflation of public sector spending – ruled out? *Wrong! The Manifesto said, "Labour will also promote an expansion in housing, the health service, education and other social services which have such a crucial part to play in providing jobs as well as in meeting vital social needs."* (Page 11.)
3. Substantial cuts in arms expenditure – ruled out? *Wrong! The Manifesto said, "We shall continue with our plans to reduce the proportion of the nation's resources devoted to defence."* (Page 37.)
4. The immediate introduction of a Wealth Tax – ruled out? *Wrong! The Manifesto said, "In the next Parliament, we shall introduce an annual Wealth Tax . . . "* (Page 14.)
5. The imposition of selected import controls – ruled out?

164

Wrong! The Manifesto said, "We shall not allow our industries to be wiped out by excessive imports before they have had a chance to recover their strength, the Labour Government will ensure that imports enter our market only within acceptable limits." (Page 11.)

It is true that the abolition of the House of Lords was not included in the Manifesto. I will tell you why. Firstly, it is impossible to create 1,000 peers in a week – to pretend so is to insult people's intelligence. If we have to abolish the Lords it would have to have been done early in the life of a new Labour Government, it would have taken two years because of the provisions of the Parliament Act, it would have been all on the Floor of the House as a major constitutional measure, and during those two years precious little else could have been done. I ask you, comrades, what would the people of this country have thought if, faced with all the economic, employment and social problems of this country, we had ignored these problems and spent the first two years abolishing the Lords? The unemployed, those wanting homes, those on hospital waiting lists, somehow I suspect they would not really appreciate this order of priority. We did put in the Manifesto the abolition of the delaying powers of the Lords, an essential first step to total abolition, which I support, but of course this is never mentioned by our critics.

Major constitutional matters cannot be dealt with overnight, it took us two years to put through the devolution legislation, which was Party policy and, I may say, some of the strongest opposition to this came from some Members of the National Executive. There are some who advocate that Abolition of the Lords should be the first priority of the new Labour Government. Is this sensible? With unemployment estimated to be 3.5 million in 1984, this seems to me to be a strange priority and not one which I think the unemployed workers would understand. I believe that they will be more concerned with getting a government devoting its time and efforts to creating thousands of jobs, rather than a thousand peers.

The motto of this union is 'Unity is Strength'. This is not a cosmetic phrase conjured up to adorn badges and banners, it is a phrase born out of bitter experience in the Labour movement over a long period of time, that if we do not stand together, fight together and work together and if we do not use every ounce of our traditional characteristics of tolerance and compassion, without doubt our enemies, who are numerous, will overwhelm us.

The year ahead will be difficult but with unity and our avowed loyalty and support for Michael Foot, our Movement will once again prove to be the only hope for millions of our fellow citizens suffering from the effects of Thatcherism. I ask that this Union Congress, together with its parliamentary representatives and the general membership, here in Brighton – give the lead and the example to the British people that will ultimately result in the restoration of a Labour Government.'

APPENDIX III

'How to Select or Reselect Your MP'

This booklet, as we saw, is a travesty. Its checklist explains how Hansard contains the voting records of MPs. It then goes on to say that the dates of debates on ten crucial issues since 1975 are listed to help Labour Party members find out the views of their own MPs on these issues. These are the issues, with my comments attached:

1. 9 April 1975, EEC membership.
   This was on the renegotiated terms for EEC membership. I think the inclusion of this vote is fair. Jim Callaghan, as Foreign Secretary, had renegotiated the best deal he could but the Parliamentary Labour Party was split from stem to stern. A free vote was allowed for Labour MPs and I voted against the terms, along with many others. The Government won comfortably with Conservative support. The voting figures were 396-170.
2. 22 July 1975, £6 pay policy.
   In actual fact there were two votes on this date. The Labour Government tabled a motion to approve the White Paper entitled 'The Attack on Inflation' (Cmd. Paper 6151). The Conservatives tabled an amendment which was defeated by 327-269. There was then a vote on the motion itself, which the Government won by 262-54. The 54 was made up of Labour backbenchers, Nationalist and Ulster MPs, and two backbench Conservatives. Officially the

Conservatives and Liberals abstained. Mullin does not explain which vote he regards as crucial.

3. 21 December 1976, Government Economic Policies following IMF loan.

A vote on the motion for the adjournment, a technical way of mounting a debate. Labour's Government won by 219 votes to 51. The Conservatives abstained, and the 51 consisted of Labour backbenchers, Nationalists and Liberals. Mullin doesn't make clear whether it was crucial to vote for or against the Labour Government.

4. 3 May 1977, Agee and Hosenball Case.

Took place at night on question of the journalists Agee and Hosenball. Again on the adjournment. The Conservatives abstained, and the Labour Government won 138-34. The 34 against were Labour backbenchers. Crucial? Mullin doesn't make it clear whether it was crucial to vote for or against the Labour Government.

5. 1 February 1979, Rhodesian Oil Sanctions.

There were four votes here, on amendments to the Labour Government motion setting up a committee to investigate allegations of breaking oil sanctions against Rhodesia. The Government won with varying majorities. The votes against the Government came from backbench Labour MPs, together with some backbench Conservatives, plus Liberals. Officially, the Conservatives abstained. Mullin doesn't explain whether he expected Labour MPs to have supported the Labour Government, or sided with the dissident Tory backbenchers.

6. 27 March 1979, Defence Expenditure.

There were two votes. The first was on an amendment to the Labour Government's motion approving its defence policy set out in the Defence Estimates 1979. The amendment was defeated by 228 votes to 52. Apart from 7 Nationalists, the remainder of the 52 were Labour backbenchers. On the main question, the Government won by 290-259, with the Conservatives voting against. Mullin does not explain which vote was crucial. Maybe he would have liked MPs to have been one of the 52 Labour backbenchers rebelling against the Government – despite the fact that the following day was scheduled for the crucial vote of confidence which finally brought down the Labour Government!

7. 13 July 1979, Corrie Abortion Bill.

This was to vote on the second reading of the Bill. Carried 242-98. This has traditionally been a matter of conscience, though some now would like to order MPs' consciences to obey Party policy.

8. 6 May 1980, Abolition of the House of Lords.

A Ten Minute Rule Bill introduced by Jeff Rooker (Labour MP, Perry Barr, Birmingham). The reader will recall these Bills rarely reach the Statute Book. It was defeated by 142 votes to 240. These Bills are not officially whipped. Nevertheless, if a Labour MP wasn't there at 4.32 pm, presumably it's a black mark in the Mullin book.

9. 4 March 1980, Continuation of Prevention of Terrorism (Temporary Provisions) Act 1976.

Conservative Government motion to approve an order for continuation of the Act. Carried 115 to 26. The 115 was Conservatives with 3 Labour; the 26 was 24 Labour MPs, plus Gerry Fitt (SDLP) and a Liberal. If this was a crucial vote, only a total of 27 Labour MPs took part, plus two Labour tellers. It makes one wonder what the criteria for choosing these votes really was. Officially, Labour was not whipped.

10. 10 December 1980, Northern Ireland Emergency Provisions.

Again a renewal of a Northern Ireland order on Emergency Provisions by the Conservative Government. Carried by 93 votes, including one Labour MP, to 21-(20 Labour backbenchers, plus Gerry Fitt). The same remarks apply to this vote as to vote 9 above.

The reader will have noticed that the earlier votes took place when the Labour Government was struggling for its existence. Frequently Labour MPs had to be kept out of their beds to beat off rebellions by Labour backbenchers, when the Conservative MPs had gone home. Presumably the Campaign for Labour Democracy, who published the booklet, and Chris Mullin, think this is a good thing. Perhaps one day we may have a fuller explanation of the so-called 'crucial issues'.

Meanwhile, since the booklet's publication that is, who knows just how many conscientious Labour MPs have been tormented with this checklist by their local Labour parties.

INDEX

abortion, 30, 37, 141, 169
Aitkin, John, 145
Allen, Leonard, 17
Allison, Peter, 55
Alton, David, 132
Apps, Ray, 109
Ashton, Joe, 108
Asquith, H.H., 14
Atomic Energy Authority, 60, 89
Attlee, Clement, 9, 10, 11, 18, 26,
    72, 97, 152

Baker, Kenneth, 86
Barker, Ben, 121, 139, 142
Basnett, David, 160, 164
Beckingham, Bryan, 130-31
Beith, Alan, 94
Benn, Anthony Wedgwood
    responsibility for Labour
        Party's decline, 8, 73, 74, 83,
        139, 152-3, 154-5
    Commons record (speaking,
        questions, committee
        attendances), 28-31, 38-40
    changes in views of, 30, 36, 37,
        41, 42, 63, 70, 82, 91, 100, 151,
        154
    views of:
        on civil service, 150-51
        on economy, 80, 97
        on electoral reform, 54
        on European Economic
            Community (EEC), 63, 70,
            75, 86-88, 90, 97, 151, 159
    on Falklands War, 97-99, 139
    on House of Lords reform,
        40-42, 80
    on immigration, 64-66
    on industrial relations, 62, 64,
        69-70, 148-49
    on Militant Tendency, 129, 132
    on monarchy, 56-57
    on nationalization, 75, 82,
        84-85, 105
    on Northern Ireland, 77
    on nuclear energy, 60-61, 66,
        91-92, 100, 151
    on nuclear weapons, 34, 36-37,
        38, 42, 77
    on party discipline and
        collective responsibility, 30,
        37, 77-8, 82, 86-7, 93-4, 97,
        119
    on press and broadcasting,
        31-32, 97, 99, 152-53
    on private education, 50
    on reselection of Labour MPs,
        46, 113, 115, 118-9, 133-4
career of: selection as candidate for
Bristol South East by-election,
13-17, 45, 111; candidate in Bristol
South East by-election (1950),
17-19; enters House of Commons,
28; early back-bench career
(1950-57). 28-35; defeat in 1954
shadow cabinet elections, 34;
spokesman on RAF, 34-38; first
elected to NEC (1959), 38; first

171

elected to Shadow Cabinet (1959), 42; Transport spokesman, 42-44; efforts to renounce peerage, 14, 44-54; disqualification from House of Commons, 49; fights Bristol South East by-election (1961), 49-51; fights Bristol South East by-election and returns to Commons (1963), 52; as Post Master General (1964-66), 56-59; as Minister of Technology (1966-70), 59-64; as Opposition Industry spokesman (1970-74), 66-7; stands for deputy leadership (1971), 68; became Chairman of the Labour Party (1971), 69; as Secretary of State for Industry (1974-75), 84-6, 88-9, 93; as Secretary of State for Energy (1975-79), 88-95; attempts to change the method for electing the Labour leader, 71-3, 96; stands for leadership (1976), 152; as chairman of NEC Home Policy Committee, 72, 99, 161; in 1980 Shadow Cabinet elections, 74; 1980 Labour conference speech on 1979 Labour Manifesto and Labour Party democracy, 74-76, 79-80, 157-61; stands for deputy leadership (1981), 76-81, 139; loses Shadow Cabinet election (1981), 82; selection as candidate for Bristol East rather than Bristol South (1983), 100, 125-8, 146; loses 1983 general election, 100, 128, 147; elected MP for Chesterfield, 148; involvement in coal dispute and Wapping dispute (1984-5), 148-9
Benn, Major John Andrews, 13-14
Bennett, Andrew, 90
Berry, Tony, 148
Bevan, Andy, 134
Bevan, Aneurin, 151
Bevin, Ernest, 13, 37
Birmingham bombers, 150
Bishop, Cllr. Ted, 12, 13, 49
Blackett, Prof., 51
Bloom, Helen, 83
Bokassa, Emperor, 87
Boundary Commission and redistribution of seats, 123, 124
Boyle, Edward, 16

Bristol, 9, 10, 21-24, 26-27, 63, 69, 81, 126-7
Bristol riots, 99
Bristol South Constituency Labour Party, 7, 24, 25, 98, 107-8, 110, 111, 118, 120-8, 133, 135, 138-46, 147
Bristol South East Constituency Labour Party, 12-19, 47-8, 49, 111, 113-5, 118, 119, 124, 127, 130, 134
British Broadcasting Corporation (BBC), 31, 97
British Leyland, 85
Brittan, Leon, 148
Brockway, Fenner, 30, 51
Bromley, Ray, 22-23
Brown, George, 68
Butler, Rab, 51
by-elections
  Bristol South East (1950), 12-19 *passim*, 50
  Bristol West (1957), 15
  Bristol South East (1961), 49-51
  Bristol South East (1963), 52
  Liverpool Edge Hill (1979), 131-32
  Chesterfield (1984), 148
  Greenwich (1987), 7, 117

Callaghan, James, 25, 71, 72, 74, 92, 93, 94, 159, 167
Cameron, James, 51
Campaign for Labour Party Democracy, 115, 119, 169-70
Campaign for Nuclear Disarmament (CND), 36-37
Carr, Robert, 64
Carter, Jimmy, 98
Castle, Barbara, 17, 86
Central Office of Information, 33
Charles, Prince, 57
Chesterfield constituency, 148
Churchill, Winston, 10, 47, 152
Civil Service, 150
coal industry, 61, 66-67, 84, 89, 148-9
Cocks, Michael
  career of in Labour Party, 20-27, 112, 123
  as Labour chief whip (1976-1985), 7, 25-26, 32, 38, 79-80, 92-94, 129, 131, 135, 140, 143-4, 162

House of Commons voting and attendance record of, 122, 140-1

selection of as candidate for Bristol South (1983), 118, 122-28

deselection of in Bristol South (1986), 7, 25-26, 95, 107-8, 138-46

condemns membership of Home Policy Committee, 72

views of on constitutional reform in the Labour Party, 71-73, 104-19 *passim*, 155

1981 speech at GMWU Congress defending 1974-79 Labour Government and 1979 Labour Manifesto, 79-80, 162-66

role of in 1981 deputy leadership election, 78-81

advocates 'no' vote in EEC referendum, 87

attitude of towards Militant Tendency and other extremists, 129-37, 150

Cocks, Valerie, 144, 147

Concannon, Don, 25

Concorde, 23, 62-63, 66

Confederation of British Industry (CBI), 89

Conservative Party, 17, 18, 19, 33, 51, 52, 55, 56, 58, 64-66, 74, 86, 90, 97, 105, 116, 124, 139, 148, 155

Cook, Robin, 126-7

Cooke, Robin, 40

Court Line, 85

Cousins, Frank, 59

Cripps, Sir Stafford, 10-15, *passim*, 17, 28

Crosland, Susan, 16

Crosland, Tony, 16-17, 51

Crossman, Richard, 51

Culverwell, C.T., 10

Cunningham, George, 117

Dalton, Hugh, 10, 17, 45

defence policy, *see also* Falklands War, 30, 36, 37, 38, 42, 79, 104, 168

Diana, Princess, 57

Douglas-Home, Sir Alec, 54

Duffy, Terry, 73

electricity industry, 58, 89, 91, 94, *see also* nuclear energy, *see* coal industry; electricity industry; gas industry; nuclear energy; oil industry; standing charges

European Economic Community (EEC), 60, 63, 70, 75, 86-88, 90, 97, 151, 167

referendum on, 86-87

Evans, Fred, 26

Evans, Moss, 160

Fabian Society, 38-39

Falklands War, 97-99, 139

Farthing Walter, 12, 13

Foot, Michael, 17, 50, 68, 74, 76, 78, 82, 83, 86, 100, 134, 166

Fyffe, Ken, 122

Gaitskell, Hugh, 42, 49, 51, 72, 97

gas industry, 58, 89, 91, 94

General and Municipal Workers' Union (GMWU), 75, 76, 79, 81, 160, 162, 164

general elections and general election manifestoes,
1945, 9
1950, 12
1951, 18, 108, 162
1959, 21, 42, 55
1964, 23, 54, 56
1966, 23-24, 59, 83
1970, 24, 62, 63, 64-66, 68
1974 (Feb. and Oct.), 84, 124, 153-4, 162
1979, 74, 79-80, 87, 95, 120, 131, 153, 164-65
1983, 82-83, 100, 134, 139-40
1987, 104, 106

Germany, 9, 10, 46

Gilby, Bill, 126

Glyn, Sir Ralph, 28

Grant, John, 24

Grimond, Jo, 51

Harris, Kenneth, 16

Harrison, Terry, 132

Harrison, Walter, 94

Hart, Judith, 98, 139

Hattersley, Roy, 128

Hatton, Derek, 109

Hayward, Ron, 113

Heald, Sir Lionel, 51
Healey, Denis, 76, 79, 81, 82, 139
Heath, Edward, 26, 64, 65, 66, 67, 84
Hinchingbrooke, Viscount, 45
Hodgkinson, Sue, 122
Hooley, Frank, 90, 117
Home Policy Committee (of NEC), 71, 72, 99, 161
Hooper, Keith, 18
Hopkins, Philip, 51
House of Lords reform, 40-42, 75-76, 80, 165, 169, see also peerages, hereditary

immigration and race relations, 64-65
Industrial Relations Act (1971), 69, 88, 162
Industry Bill (1974-5), 84-85, 88
International Monetary Fund (IMF), 97

Jackson, Vic, 120
Jenkin, Patrick, 90
Jenkins, Roy, 68
Johnson, Walter, 24
Jones, Arthur Creech, 12, 13, 15, 16
Joseph, Sir Keith, 64

Kaufman, Gerald, 25
Khama, Seretse, 30
Khomeni, Ayatollah, 98
King, Horace, 17
King, Tom, 92
Kinnock, Neil, 7, 8, 74, 81, 128
Kitson, Alex, 76
Knight, Ted, 113

Labour Governments, 151, 152, 160-61,
1945-51, 9-10, 152
1964-66, 56-59
1966-70, passim 59-66
1974-79, 25, 84, 163
Labour Party, (The Labour Party is mentioned throughout the book, but references to specific key categories are given here)
constitution of, 8, 56, 71-4, 134, 152, 155, 165, 167-70
internal fighting in, 56, 68-83,

passim, 104, 139, 153, 154, 162, 165-66 see also Militant Tendency
leadership and deputy leadership elections in, 56, 68, 71-74, 133, 155
1970, 68
1971, 68
1976, 152
1981, 76-81, 139, 146
1983, 100-101
1988, 8, 155
prospects and popularity of, (ii), 56, 104-105, 152-3. See also Benn, Anthony Wedgwood, responsibility for Labour Party's decline
See also Benn, Anthony Wedgwood; Bristol South Constituency Labour Party; Bristol South East Constituency Labour Party; general elections; Labour Governments; Labour Party conferences; Labour Shadow Cabinets, National Executive Committee, Reselection of Labour MPs.
Labour Party conferences, 41, 152
1960, 42
1963, 59
1974, 115
1978, 95, 108-109, 115
1979, 112
1980, 72, 74-76, 157-61
1981 (January), special Wembley conference, 73, 139
1988, 7
Labour Shadow Cabinets, 34, 42, 57, 62, 68, 70, 74, 77, 82, 96, 105
Labour Weekly, 153, 163
Legg, Ken, 114
Lestor, Joan, 81
Liberal Party, 14, 22, 37, 94, 95, 122, 132
Lib-Lab Pact, 94
Life Peerage Bill (1958), 39, 40
Life Peerage Act (1963), 48, 52
Livingstone, Ken, 113
Llewellyn Davies, Richard, 51
Lloyd, Mrs M.P., 52
Local Government Reorganization

Act (1972), 112
'London Factor', 117
London Labour Briefing, 113
Lyons, Alex, 160

MacGregor, Ian, 148-9
Macmillan, Harold, 22
mandatory reselection, *see*
   reselection of Labour MPs
manifestos, Labour, *see under*
   Labour Party, constitution of;
   general elections (especially 1974
   and 1979)
Marsh, Richard, 51
Martell, Edward, 52
Mason, Alan, 147
Mason, Anne, 120
Martin, Cllr. Tom, 49
May, Andrew, 120, 122-23, 145
Mayhew, Christopher, 152
Mclaren, Cllr. John, 114, 130, 131
McWatters, George, 17
Mellish, Bob, 24-25, 86
metric system, 63
Micklewright, George, 121, 122
Mikardo, Ian, 118
Militant Tendency, 109, 112, 114,
   129-37, 152
Morgan, Trevor, 122
Muggeridge, Malcolm, 51
Mulley, Fred, 117
Mullin, Chris, 13, 119, 150, 167-70

National Enterprise Board, 84-85
National Executive Committee
   (NEC), 32, 38, 49, 71, 72, 78, 82,
   93-4, 99, 110, 115, 116, 118, 131,
   132, 136, 141, 142, 153-61 *passim*
   see also Home Policy Committee
National Union of Mineworkers
   (NUM), 61, 66-7
New Bristol Group, 53-54
Nichol, Mrs M.E., 13, 16
Northern Ireland, 77
nuclear energy, 60-61, 66, 89, 91-2,
   100, 151

oil industry, 89, 90, 163
Orme, Stanley, 81

Paget, Reggie, 45
Palmer, Arthur, 68, 69, 81, 92,
   113-15, 123, 130
Pannell, Charles, 48, 51
Party Political Broadcasts, 31-32
Pavitt, Laurie, 110
Pearl, G. 52
Peart, Fred, 68
Peglar, Cllr. Bert, 48
peerages, hereditary, 40, 45-54
Peerages, Renunciation Bill (1961),
   48
Pentonville Five, 69
Petersen, Prof, 51
Phillips, Morgan, 21
Pidgeon, Fred, 120
Powell, Enoch, 64-65
pressure groups, 42-43, 91
Primarolo, Dawn, 95, 138, 142,
   145, 147
Pym, Francis, 25

Rank and File Mobilizing
   Committee, 77
reselection of Labour MPs, 7, 12,
   46, 104-19, 133-4, 167-70, *see
   also* under Cocks, Michael;
   deselection in Bristol South
Revolutionary Socialist League, 129
Rio Tinto Zinc, 90
Rippon, Geoffrey, 99
Rodgers, Bill, 74
Rolls Royce, 66
Rooker, Jeff, 169

St Clair, Malcolm, 51-52
Sands, Robert, 77
Sedgemore, Brian, 92-93
Shaw, George Bernard, 39
shipbuilding industry, 60-62, 69-70,
   85, 163
Shipbuilding Industry Bill, 61-62
Shipbuilding Industry Board, 62
Shore, Peter, 86
Silkin, John, 76, 81, 86, 139
Social Democratic Party (SDP), 24,
   54, 117, 152
Soper, Donald, 51
stamps, postage, 56-57
Stanley, Col. Oliver, 10
Stansgate, Viscount (Anthony
   Wedgwood Benn's father), 14-15,
   28, 29, 30-31, 44, 47, 52
Stansgate Titles Deprivation Bill, 46

Stephen, Jessie, 70
Stockwood, Rt. Rev. Mervyn (Bishop of Southwark), 17
Suez Crisis, 33

Tatlow, Cllr. Pam, 145
Tebbit, Norman, 86
television licenses, 58
Thatcher, Margaret, 66, 98, 100
Titles Deprivation Act (1917), 46
Transport and General Workers' Union, 13, 59, 158, 160

Ungoed-Thomas, Sir Lynn, 48
Upper Clyde Shipbuilders, 62
Urquhart, Beryl, 20, 65
USA, 11, 16, 36, 66, 70
USSR, 10, 30, 36, 70

Varley, Eric, 89, 148

Wall, Pat, 109

Walton, Bob, 121
Wapping printing dispute, 149-50
Warburton, David, 158, 164
Webb, Sidney and Beatrice, 39
Wedgwood Benn (Renunciation Bill), 47
Wellbeloved, James, 25
Wembley Conference (Jan. 1981), 73, 139
Wilkins, Christine, 142, 143
Wilkins, Will, 24, 26, 48, 68, 123
Williams, Len, 15
Willmott, Cllr. Roy, 24, 121
Wilson, Harold, 25, 51, 56, 59, 64, 65, 72, 77, 84, 85, 89, 93
Windle, Dick, 15
Windscale, 66, 92
Woods, Marilyn, 121
Wright, Peter, 150

Young Socialists, 55, 134, 155